E. W. KENYON
Author
(1867-1948)

Sixteenth Printing

ISBN 1-57770-003-1

New Creation

Realities

– A Revelation of Redemption –

BY

E.W. KENYON

CONTENTS

FIRST WORDS

SERIES of heart messages on the New Creation Realities. Little studies on great themes. Investigations about the "Hidden man of the Heart." We have found the secret that the psychologists long have sought.

It is "the inward man"; it is the Recreated spirit; it is the part of man with which God deals.

A delving into the love life of the sons of Love, where the "hidden man of the heart" rules the outer or seen man of the senses.

You will find some suggestions about the combat of the Recreated spirit with the senses which govern this outer man.

It is really an unveiling of what we are in Christ today; of what He says we are; what He has made us to be in His great Redemptive work.

These messages are largely from the Epistles.

They are not complete, but are suggestions to provoke you to study more deeply in these hidden riches.

We have come to know that one cannot know the Incarnate One as we have seen Him in the four Gospels, unless we have had an opportunity to become acquainted with Him in the Epistles.

In the Gospels He is the Lone Man of Galilee, the humble Unknown, who ends His earth walk on Calvary.

In the Epistles He is the Risen, Triumphant One, the conqueror of death, sin and Satan.

He is humanity's Risen Redeemer who has met the demands of Justice and satisfied every claim against humanity.

He made possible the New Creation, a new race of men, who can stand in God's presence without the sense of guilt, condemnation or inferiority.

THE REASON WHY

The Pauline Epistles must ever stand as the work of a super-genius or a divine revelation.

They reveal what happened on the cross and what followed during the three days and three nights until the Man was raised from the dead.

One cannot grasp the great Substitutionary fact in the four Gospels.

Neither can we find the New Creation Revelation; nor can we discover the ministry of Jesus at the right hand of the Father.

The four Gospels give us a sense knowledge view of the Man.

The people stood in the presence of His miracles, overwhelmed with a consciousness that they were in the presence of God.

They call Him the Son of God.

They see Him conquer Satan and demons, but there is no intimation that He is going to make them conquerors of demons, of death and of disease.

What He says to them in regard to it is veiled because they are spiritually unable to grasp spiritual realities.

They have not yet experienced the strange phenomena of the New Birth.

So the Pauline Revelation is a master stroke of Divine Grace.

It lets us into the inner secret of God's mighty purpose in the incarnation.

In the Gospels Jesus acts like Deity, talks like Deity, dies like Deity, and conquers death like God.

He was God manifest in the flesh in His earth walk and He was God in the Spirit in His Substitutionary sacrifice.

At God's right hand He has a glorified body and is Head of the New Creation.

You will find that He did a perfect work for us and the Spirit through the Word does a perfect work in us as Jesus is today at the right hand of the Father doing a perfect work for us.

Chapter I

THE LIVING WORD

UR attitude toward the Word determines the place that God holds in our daily life.

The Word should always be the Father speaking to us. It should never be like the message from an ordinary book.

It should be as real to you as though the Master stood in the room and spoke to you personally.

This Word was designed by the Father to take Jesus' place in His absence.

When He says, "The Father Himself loveth you," it is a personal message to your heart.

When the Master said again, "If a man loves me, he will keep my word; and the Father and I will love him and make our home with him," that should be as personal as though you were the only one in the world.

It is as though you were sitting at the feet of Jesus, and He looked down into your face and said, "The Father and I will come and make our home with you.

"Be not dismayed, for I am your God.

"I am going to be your strength; I am going to lend to you my own ability.

"When weakness comes, remember that I am the strength of your life.

"When you need finances, remember that I said, 'My Father knoweth that you have need of all these things'."

You can whisper to your own heart, "My Father will supply every need of mine. He knows my needs and loves me. He and I are one."

Man's word is usually dead before the printer has finished his work. Few words of man live after a generation, but God's Word is different. It is impregnated with the very Life of God, it is eternal.

Heb. 4:12,13 gives us an illustration: (Moffatt's Translation) "For the Logos of God is a living thing, active and more cutting than any sword with double edge, penetrating to the very division of soul and spirit, joints and marrow - scrutinizing the very thoughts and conceptions of the heart. And no created thing is hidden from him; all things lie open and exposed before the eyes of him with whom we have to reckon."

This is one of the strangest statements about the Word in Paul's

Epistles.

Notice this 13th verse: "That no created thing is hidden from him."

Of whom is he speaking? The Living Word – The Logos.

"And all things lie open and exposed before the eyes of him with whom we have to do."

The Word takes on personality; it becomes Christ Himself.

Our contact with the Master, then, is through His Word.

And did you notice, "the eyes of Him." The Word then has eyes. It sees our conduct, our attitude toward it. It is a Living thing.

How deeply that should impress us.

I hold in my hands a Book with the very Life of God in it, a Book that scrutinizes my conduct; that judges me.

A Book that feeds this inner man – my spirit.

It imparts Faith to my Spirit, builds Love into it.

God's only means of reaching me is through His Word. So the Word becomes a vital thing.

It has been rather difficult for some of us to grasp the fact that during the first century, the Christian Church did not have our New Testament.

The first epistle that Paul wrote to the Thessalonians was the beginning of the New Testament. It was written seventeen years after his conversion.

I Thess. 2:13, "Wherefore I also give continual thanks to God, because, when you heard from me the Spoken Word of God, you received it not as the word of man, but, as it is in truth, the Word of God; who Himself works effectually in you that believe." (Conybeare).

Notice, it was "the Spoken Word." That was all they had … whether Paul gave it, or Peter, or John, or any of the Apostles.

It was God speaking through human lips.

It had not yet been put into writing.

Now you can better understand Acts 19:20 telling of that great revival at Ephesus.

Luke used this expression: "So mightily grew the Word of the Lord and prevailed."

It was the Spoken Word.

The Pauline Relevation was only known to those who had heard him.

The other Apostles did not have it. They had what the Spirit gave them to meet the emergency of the hour.

It is a fact that Christianity is what the Word says about

Redemption, about the Body of Christ, or the New Creation.

We become Christlike in the measure that the Word prevails in us.

The Word is Christ revealed.

The Word is God present with us, speaking the Living Message of the Loving Father God.

The Word is always NOW.

It is His Word to me today. It is His voice, His last message.

It becomes a Living thing in my heart as I lovingly act upon it.

It becomes a Living thing on the lips of Love.

It has no power on the lips of those whose lives are out of fellowship with Him, who live in the reason realm.

His Word makes our ministry limitless.

His Word is what He is.

It is the mind of the Father.

It is the Will of the Father.

It shows the way to the Father.

The Word is the Father speaking.

You notice that it is always in the present tense.

The Word is the Bread of Heaven, food for our spirits.

Matt. 4:4, "Man shall not live by bread alone, but by every word that proceedeth out of the mouth of God."

Jer. 15:16 says, "Thy words were found, and I did eat them. Thy words were unto me a joy and rejoicing of my heart."

Job tells us how precious the Word is to him. Job 23:12: "I have not gone back from the commandment of his lips; I have treasured up the words of his mouth more than my necessary food."

When a child of God looks upon the Word as Job did, then it becomes a Reality in his daily life.

Job had no Written Word; he had the Word spoken by angels.

We have the Written Word.

We have it printed in many forms so we may carry it in our pocket.

How little we have appreciated the value of His message.

Psa. 107:20 "He sent His Word and healed them."

That Living Word that He sent was Jesus.

Mark 16:19-20: "So then the Lord Jesus, after he had spoken unto them, was received up into heaven, and sat down at the right hand of God. And they went forth, and preached everywhere, the Lord working with them, and confirming the word by the signs that followed."

Notice that the Lord worked with them.

5

I believe that a revival would break out almost anywhere if the Lord worked with those who preach, and if the Word was as real to them as the Spoken Word was real to the Early Church.

But the word of man has gained the ascendancy and has more authority than His Word has today.

He confirms the Word today everywhere that it is preached.

I want you to notice how the Father makes the Word good in the lives of men and women as they dare to act upon it.

In the closing sentence of the Gospel of Matthew, "Lo, I am with you always, even unto the end of the age," the believer can be sure that though he be forsaken by all others, there is One who will stand by him.

But the thing that has most deeply impressed my heart is the Reality of God in the Word.

He is not only in the Word, but He breathes His very life through it as it is unfolded.

He said, "Where two or three are gathered together in my name, there am I in the midst of them."

He is in the midst of them in the Word.

Jesus said, "If ye love me, the Father and I will come and make our home with you" (John 14:23).

If we could only realize that when we open the Word, it is a Living Thing we are implanting in the hearts of men.

The Word is God present with us speaking the Living Message of the Living Father God.

It is the NOW Word from Him to me. It is His voice.

It becomes a living thing in the heart of Faith.

In Rom. 10:8 it is called the "Word of Faith."

It is His Word that gives birth to faith in the believer. It is God's faith expressed.

You see, He is a Faith God and He always uses words to do things.

Heb. 11:3 "By faith we understand that the worlds have been framed by the Word of God."

Hear Him whisper, "By myself have I sworn" (Gen. 22:16).

He was in the Word. The Word was a part of Him.

You can't separate a man from his words; neither can you separate the Father from His Words.

How it thrilled me when I read in Heb. 7:22 that Jesus is the surety of the New Covenant.

The New Covenant is the Word, and He is the surety of the Word.

The Word was a living fact when Jesus spoke it. It is still a living fact.

Jesus was a part of all He said; He and His Word were one.

Jesus is just as real now as He was the day He arose from the dead.

His Word is just as real now as when He inspired John or Peter or Paul to write it.

What He said was a part of Himself.

Reality throbs in it, flows through it, lives in it.

The Word was; the Word is now what it was then.

Here are some other assurances:

Psa. 23:1, "The Lord is my shepherd."

John 10:14, Jesus said, "I am the good shepherd."

Isa. 41:10, "Fear thou not, for I am with thee: be not dismayed, for I am thy God."

Rom. 8:31, "If God is for you, who can be against you?"

Phil. 4:13, "I can do all things in him who strengtheneth me."

Psa. 27:1, "God is the strength of my life, of whom shall I be afraid?"

Phil. 4:19, "My God shall supply every need of yours according to his riches in glory in Christ Jesus."

Psa. 121:1,2, "My help cometh from the Lord."

Psa. 84:5, "My strength is in Him."

Psa. 62:5-8, "God is my refuge."

These are Living Words, and as you feed on them they build you up.

The knowledge of what Christ is and has done for you personally, builds faith in you.

When I turn to the Word and read it as His message to me, He confirms that message in my life.

He confirmed the covenant made with Abraham.

He confirmed the Word that Jesus spoke through the Apostles. (Mark 16:20).

Jesus said in John 14:15, "If ye love me, ye will keep my commandments."

What was His commandment? That we love one another.

He that loveth me and keepeth My Word, he it is, you see, that the Father loves.

Here are some other facts that we ought to remember.

John 16:8,9, "When He (the Spirit) is come, He will convict the world of sin, of righteousness and of judgment: of sin, because they believe not on Me; of righteousness, because I go unto the Father;

of judgment, because the prince of this world is judged."

What is going to convince the world?

Words in the lips of Faith.

Only that Living Word in the lips of Faith can take the place of an absent Christ.

The Word talks to us. It takes the place of Jesus.

The Word is the Father speaking to us now.

It has the same authority that it would have if the Master stood in the room and spoke it.

Faith in the Father is Faith in His Word.

The Word takes on all that our Faith demands.

Jesus said, "According to your faith, so be it unto you."

As you consider the Word and act upon it, it will become real to you.

This Book, the Living Word, has God in it.

The Word takes the place of the unseen Jesus.

Meditation in the Word is like a visit with Jesus.

Josh. 1:8, God told Joshua to meditate in the Word day and night; in other words, to live in it.

Jesus said in John 8:31 "Abide in my word."

The Word gets into your blood, into your system and becomes a part of you.

The Word is inspired. Holy men spoke as they were moved by the Holy Spirit, as they were borne along in their spirit life.

God spoke by the mouth of the holy prophets.

"The words that I speak unto you, they are spirit and they are life."

Every word that God speaks has life in it.

Remember Heb. 4:12: "The *Logos* of God is a Living Thing."

It is not like man's words which die after a generation; God's Word lives.

I love to think of it as the "prevailing Word," as it was in Ephesus. How it ruled over that wicked city!

Today the Logos of God is ruling in the hearts of those who yield to its sway.

The Word has the authority of God in it now.

It has the Righteousness of God in it.

It has Recreating power for the unsaved.

It has healing power for the sick.

It is the very Bread of Heaven to the hungry in spirit.

I wish that it could be like this: that when you pick up the Word

8

it will mean that God is present with you and that the Word is His attitude toward you now.

It is His attitude toward sin, toward Redemption, toward Righteousness, toward Eternal Life, toward the Sons and Daughters of God.

That is the Father's attitude toward all the issues of life.

My word is my will. The Word is the Will of the Father.

God watches over His Word.

What God says is, becomes.

God is Truth, so I will be true.

God is Light, so I will walk in the Light.

You see, we learn to act on the Word, as we act on the word of a banker or a lawyer in some crisis in our life.

I wonder if you ever realized that the Father is jealous over His Word.

He never set a low estimate upon it. He holds it in the highest regard.

If He said it, that ends it.

To His enemies, it is but paper and ink; but to the Lovers, it is Life and health; it is joy unspeakable.

The preaching that produces little conviction, is caused by the Word not having been in the heart of the teacher.

We are to be sowers of the Word.

Jesus gave us in Matt. 13 a marvelous picture of the art of preaching.

It is sowing the Word. It falls upon all kinds of hearts, but the irrigation of the soil is dependent upon the sower.

If we irrigate it with prayer and sometimes with tears, it is bound to bring forth a harvest.

Some of us forget the Word in hard places.

Unconsciously we walk by sight. The senses take the reality away from the Word, but as the spirit gains the ascendancy over the senses, the Word once more has its place.

Remember, your word is you. You must learn to say, "I gave my word; I must keep it, no matter what it costs."

If your word is of no value, you will reason that the Word of God is of no value.

I have found that unbelief in the Word of God is largely because of people's lack of faith in their own word.

If you want to build the highest type of faith, be a faithful person yourself. Believe in your own word.

9

Establish a reputation for truth; then the Word will be that to you in your life.

Here are some little facts that may mean much to your life.

The Word is on my hands. What am I going to do with it?

Am I going to act upon it, let it govern my life, or will I just study it?

Will I sit in the Bible class and study it and then go back to my room and study it but not live it? Not let it become a part of my life, but just an intellectual exercise?

The Word is taking the Master's place in my life.

What I do with the Word will determine what the Word will do to me one of these days.

The Word will work in me, building Jesus' life in me, building Life, Faith, Love, Grace and strength into me, or else it will judge me in the last day.

What will it do for me? It will work for me.

If I preach it and live it, it will work for me. It will reveal the very riches of my inheritance to me.

It will give me courage to enter into and enjoy my inheritance.

It will build the Master's stedfastness into me.

The very character of Christ will be built into me, and only He knows what it will do through me.

It has saved the lost; it has healed the sick; it has built faith and love in multitudes.

Let the Word of Christ then dwell in you richly.

You can so soak in the Word and the Word so soak in you, that your word and God's Word become blended into one.

It will be your language and your words, but it will be His Word.

His Word in you becomes a part of you.

It has made you what you are; it will make others like you.

You are lost in the Word, but the Word is found in you.

The Word became Flesh once. It is becoming spirit in your spirit.

The Word dwells richly in your practice, in your conversation, in your prayer, in your convictions.

You are using the Word to cast out diseases, to bring money to people, to save lost souls.

This Word and you have become one.

You remember that for more than fifty years after Christ's death, the Written Word was known only in a very limited way.

The New Testament wasn't brought together until the middle of the second century.

The Words that Jesus spoke were not yet written. It was the "Spoken Word," but He was in it. They were a part of Christ and they breathed Christ's Nature.

Remember, the Word of God liveth and abideth. All right, speak the Word and it will live in the lives of men who hear you.

He said, "I watch over my Word." He will watch over the Word you preach and teach.

Jesus said, "If my words are living in you and you are speaking them, I will live in them as they pass from your lips."

The Word of Christ becomes a Living thing in your lips.

Speak the Word fearlessly.

Let the Word live in you gloriously and richly.

Chapter II

TREATING THE WORD AS THOUGH IT WERE A COMMON BOOK

THIS title bears the heart reason for spiritual failure. It is the reason why in daily life, the believer breaks down, why the adversary has no trouble in overthrowing him in a crisis; the reason why he is a spiritual hitchhiker, always depending upon someone else's prayers, someone else's wisdom, someone else's interpretation of the Word.

He has no life of his own independent of others.

In the Family of God, he is a "yes man," but it is always, "yes" in the wrong place.

Paul describes him in Heb. 5:12. I shrink from giving you this Scripture; it is so personal in so many lives.

"For when by reason of time ye ought to be teachers, (ought to be leaders and soul-winners), ye have need again that someone teach you the very rudiments of the first principles of the oracles of God."

It is a pity, you seem to have forgotten the first steps in this Divine Life.

Instead of walking out into the fulness and liberty and riches of His grace, you have halted.

There has been no growth, no development in your life.

The Word doesn't mean much to you.

Oh, there are certain Scriptures you know that condemn you and make you feel miserable, but there is no life in the Word for you.

"The Word is a lamp unto my feet, a light unto my pathway," but it isn't that to you.

The Word hurts and cuts and bruises and makes you feel unhappy when you read it, when it should be manna and food for you.

Notice how tenderly he said, that "someone teach you the rudiments," the very beginning of the faith life.

Why? Because instead of living it, acting it, and taking your place in the Word, you have remained a babe, an undeveloped spirit.

Your mind has never been renewed by the Word. You see it can't be renewed until you begin to practice it.

Jesus hit the tap-root of it in Matt. 7:24. He said, "Every one that heareth these words of mine, and doeth them, shall be likened unto a wise man, who built his house upon the rock: and the rain descended, and the floods came, and the winds blew, and beat upon that house; and it fell not: for it was founded upon the rock. But he that heareth these words of mine, and doeth them not, is like unto the man that built his house on the sand." The first high tide swept him out into the sea.

I am sorry for such folks. They have to be fed with milk all the time. You will find them in the nursery. They always have a bottle. Some of them have the wrong bottle. It is not filled with the sincere milk of the Word.

They are babes in all their conduct.

Paul in I Cor. 3:3, "And ye are yet carnal."

That means they live in the senses; they are ruled by the senses; they are guided by the senses.

All their diseases are sense made.

He says they are walking after the manner of men, or as "mere men" of the world. Just world folks.

There has been no change, no growth, no development in their life whatever.

They are treating the Word as though it is a common book.

They can't get their healing. Others have to pray for them and they are a burden upon the Church.

They are a spiritual liability.

If they happen to be men and women of ability and of standing in the community, and the Church gives them office or a place of responsibility, they become a deadly burden to the Church.

They are never in the Bible class.

They do not have family prayer, and seldom ask the blessing at the table.

They belong to the A Class of hitch-hikers.

Their faith is always weak.

You will see them going to the altar but they never get anything.

The altar is a place for babes to get an impulse to go to the Word and feed on it.

It is not a means to an end. It is just a beginning.

But if you see them going to the altar year after year, you know they have become habitual, spiritual cripples.

Satan rules them through the senses.

They are afraid of death. They are afraid to meet the Lord.

They have thrown away Life's privileges because they lightly esteemed the Word of God.

Some Facts We Ought to Study in This Connection

When I ask another to pray for my healing or to pray for any of my chronic needs, I reject the gift of my healing, and I doubt the Word of the Giver.

I repudiate my own Righteousness in Christ, and I refuse to take my place in Christ as a Son.

I know that no one has a better standing than I have. No one has a better place in the Vine than I have.

No one can draw life from the Vine more readily than I can.

I am what He made me in Christ.

My Righteousness was given to me in Christ.

My right to the use of Jesus' name is a gift, but I have repudiated the whole thing.

I have neglected to develop my gift. I have ignored the admonition of my Lord. I do not study the Word to live it!

I know that my sickness is because of a spiritual condition.

I know that I have walked according to the senses rather than according to the Spirit.

I know that healing cannot be permanent in my body until my spirit is adjusted to the Word.

If sickness is not spiritual, He couldn't have made Christ's spirit sick with my diseases, and if my body is filled with disease, it is because my spirit is not in harmony with the Word.

I am rebelling against the sickness and fighting against the pain, but I don't fight the cause of my sickness. I fight the effect of it.

You see, until I take my place in Christ and begin to act the Word and become a doer of the Word instead of a talker, I remain a failure.

Sickness is threefold, Spiritual, Mental and Physical.

All are sick in spirit before they are sick in body!

You see, here is where the trouble is. James 1:22 tells us, "But be ye doers of the word, and not hearers only, deluding your own selves."

One can stay in that condition, until after awhile they begin to believe they are right and God is wrong, and you will hear them whining, "Why does God put these things on me?" and some unwise teacher will say, "He is trying to discipline you."

I tell you, He never uses the devil to discipline His children.

Disease is of the devil.

You are suffering the results of refusing to take your place in Christ.

14

You refuse to study to show yourself approved unto Him.

You have refused to feed on the Word.

You had opportunity to study but you didn't take it.

You would rather read the literature of the hour than to read the Word from Heaven.

The great heart of the Master is yearning over you.

His intercession has been ineffectual so far. It can't be effectual until the Word works effectively in your spirit.

You must study to show yourself approved of God.

Chapter III

THE FOUR GOSPELS IN CONTRAST WITH THE PAULINE EPISTLES

N the early days of my ministry, German philosophy had gained the ascendency in many of our theological institutions, and there came a strange new slogan.

You heard it continuously – "Back to Jesus."

It captured my imagination but I didn't know what it meant.

Then I heard one of our leaders declare that Paul had altogether too much influence over the Church, and that we are to give up the Pauline Revelation and go "back to Jesus."

That was really the beginning of my study of the Pauline Revelation.

The four Gospels, you remember, were written years after Christ's resurrection.

Luke's Gospel was written from 63 to 80 A. D.

The Gospel of John was written from 80 to 110 A.D.

That meant two generations after the resurrection of Jesus before John wrote.

From my study, I notice this strange fact, that Paul quoted Jesus only twice, and in John's Gospel there were only two traces of the Pauline Revelation.

One is John 1:16,17: "For of his fulness we all received, and grace for grace. For the law was given through Moses; grace and truth came through Jesus Christ."

I began to wonder why the four Gospels did not have any of the Pauline Revelation in them.

Then I discovered that they recorded only events up to the resurrection and ascension.

They knew what had taken place on the Day of Pentecost and of the tremendous upheaval that followed the preaching of the Apostle's in Jerusalem, Samaria, and in the Roman Empire, yet they never made mention of it.

I wondered how John could have written his Gospel as he did, knowing that he had passed through the great revival in Jerusalem; that he had been a part of all those mighty miracles until the destruction of Jerusalem, when he himself was banished from the holy land; and knowing of the miracles that had attended his ministry before he was banished to the Isle of Patmos, and yet he did not tell us any of those wonderful things that had taken place.

You remember in John 20:30,31, he declares, "Many other signs therefore did Jesus in the presence of the disciples, which are not written in this book: but these are written, that ye may believe that Jesus is the Christ, the Son of God; and that believing ye may have life in his name."

You see, the object of his writing was that we might have faith in Christ.

Then I said to John in my imagination, "Brother, why haven't you told us more about the miracles that occurred under your ministry through the name of Jesus?"

And then it seemed to me as though John answered, "I wrote only what the Holy Spirit gave me."

Then I saw one of the greatest literary miracles of all ages.

The four men who had written these Gospels, had been shut in, as it were, by the Holy Spirit.

They had been unable to give their interpretation of the miracles or what the miracles meant.

They wrote only what He had permitted, or rather, had inspired them to write.

You can't conceive of anyone writing a book like Luke or Matthew, or John or Mark who had the experiences they had, without those experiences intruding themselves into the biography of the man of whom they were written.

Here are some facts:

John didn't write for more than seventy years after the ascension of our Lord.

He must have known of the Pauline Revelation.

Paul's letters had some circulation during those two generations, and John had met Paul and had visited with him.

He had learned from the lips of Paul what Christ had done for him in His great Substitutionary Sacrifice, and yet there is no intimation of it in his Gospel.

Luke, a convert of Paul, traveled with him about eighteen years.

He had been Paul's helper and had taken care of him when he was in prison, and yet I challenge you to go through his Gospel and find one sentence that indicates that he knew anything about the Pauline Revelation.

The same thing is true of the Book of Acts.

That is another literary miracle.

Luke loved Paul. He lived in the consciousness of the finished work of Christ.

17

Christ's ministry at the right hand of the Father was one of the dearest facts of his life without doubt, and yet he never mentions it.

Mark was Paul's companion for years, yet you can see no intimation of the Substitutionary Sacrifice of Christ in his Gospel.

Let us notice some of the things that they knew but utterly ignored.

None of them mention Christ as a Substitute, the sin-bearer, the one who would put sin away by the sacrifice of Himself.

The New Creation was not developed.

John gives us the little talk that Jesus had with Nicodemus, but the Ruler of Israel did not understand it.

John had a great opportunity there to have put in what he had come to know about the New Creation.

Not a word is mentioned about Christ becoming our Righteousness, or how He was delivered up on account of our trespasses and raised when we were justified.

Not a word is mentioned about the Body of Christ. The nearest is John 15 where Jesus said, "I am the vine, ye are the branches."

What an opportunity John had then to develop the theme and how glad we would have been if he had done it.

No, God shut him in and enabled him to say exactly what He wanted him to say and nothing more.

There is nothing about the great ministry of our Master at the right hand of the Father, of His being a Mediator, Intercessor, Advocate, High Priest and Lord.

All this sums up to one tremendous fact, that when you read the four Gospels, you are standing in the presence of God Himself, unseen, but He is there.

He is the Author of those four matchless documents.

He is there unveiling His Son and the Son is unveiling Him.

In the Pauline Epistles we have the Father unveiling the work that He wrought in His Son and through Him.

He is also unveiling the Family, the Body of Christ, the Sons of God.

But we are interested in another phase of it – a contrast of the Pauline Revelation, and Jesus' teaching.

Paul's treatment of Faith is an illustration.

Jesus continually urged His hearers, the sons of that First Covenant, to believe.

In such scriptures as Mark 9:23, Jesus said, "All things are possible to him that believeth."

Again He said to His disciples in the midst of that storm on the sea, "Oh thou of little faith; wherefore didst thou doubt?"

Mark 11:23,24, "Whosover shall say unto this mountain, Be thou taken up and cast into the sea; and shall not doubt in his heart, but shall believe that what he saith cometh to pass; he shall have it.

"Therefore I say unto you, all things whatsoever ye pray and ask for, believe that ye receive them, and ye shall have them."

Why didn't Paul urge his Epistles people to believe?

He urged the unsaved to believe on Christ, but he never urged the Church to believe.

That confused me. I wondered why, for I remembered that all of our preachers and evangelists and teachers have told what we might do as believers if we only had faith.

Then I saw the secret. We are believers. We are the Sons of God.

Eph. 1:3 declares "Blessed be the God and Father of our Lord Jesus Christ, who hath blessed us with every spiritual blessing."

We are in the Family. All that the Father has and all that He wrought in Christ, and all that Christ is, belongs to us.

We don't need faith for a thing that is already ours.

The thing for which I must have faith is something that I do not possess.

I Cor. 3:21 declares, "Wherefore let no one glory in men. For all things are yours."

Whether Paul gave you the revelation of it or Peter or John, it makes no difference.

They unveiled simply what belongs to us.

Now we can understand why our modern preaching in regard to faith has been almost destructive.

(I wish you could read my book "The Two Kinds of Faith." That will illustrate what we are talking about more fully.)

Paul's Revelation gives us a perfect Redemption.

Eph. 1:7 "In whom we have our redemption through his blood, the remission of our trespasses, according to the riches of his grace."

Notice the tense here. Not, we may have it if we have faith enough; no, "In whom we have (now) our redemption through his blood," We have "the remission of our trespasses."

The Greek word does not mean "forgiveness," as it is translated; it is "remission." That comes always in the New Birth.

Forgiveness is something we get when we sin as believers.

Remission is something that the sinner gets when he comes into the Family.

19

The Greek word "aphesis" is used in Col. 1:14 (and Eph. 1:7): "In whom we have our redemption, the remission of our trespasses."

Rotherham's translation will clear it up for anyone who wishes to study the subject.

Not only have we a perfect Redemption in the Pauline Revelation, but now we can go back and stand by the side of the cross with the disciples and we can say, "Peter, do you know what Jesus is doing on the cross?

"He is being made sin now. Watch Him, and when He cries that last bitter cry and yields up His spirit, He is going to the place of suffering as your Substitute and mine. He is going to stay there until the demands of Justice are met; until Satan is conquered; until the New Birth becomes a possibility; until man can be justified, receive the Nature and Life of Deity, and become the very Righteousness of God in Christ."

Peter looks mystified. John draws near and says, "Pardon me, but what are you talking about?"

You see, they knew nothing about what Christ was doing for us.

Jesus had broken into the realm of sense knowledge, had been manifest among them as the Son of God for three and a half years, and they didn't know Him.

They didn't know what He did on the cross and what He did during the three days and three nights.

They didn't know what His resurrection meant, nor what He meant when He said to Mary to touch Him not for He had not yet ascended to the Father.

All this was unknown to them.

It is deeply important that we understand the difference between the Pauline Revelation and the ministry of Jesus and its teachings as recorded in the four Gospels.

Chapter IV

PAUL ABOUT PRAYER

AUL teaches us about prayer by his prayers.

True, in Eph. 6:18 he says, "With all prayer and supplication praying at all seasons in the Spirit, and watching thereunto in all perseverance and supplication for all saints."

You notice he uses the expression "with all prayer (or with all kinds of prayer) and supplication in the Spirit."

Whether that be in the Holy Spirit or in his recreated spirit, one can't be sure, but they would actually mean the same thing.

It suggests in I Thess. 5:17 "Pray without ceasing."

Your life becomes a continual intercession.

It is not by words, the spirit in you is doing what Paul mentions in Rom. 8:26: "And in like manner the Spirit also helpeth our infirmity: for we know not how to pray as we ought; but the Spirit himself maketh intercession for us with groanings which cannot be uttered."

I have noticed at times when I have been depressed, and I could think of no reason for the depression, that afterward I discovered it was the Spirit in me making intercession; the silent agony of the Spirit reaching out after someone.

It was my spirit blending with the Holy Spirit in supplication for some person that was in need at that hour.

When I was in evangelistic work, the day before I gave the invitation to the unsaved, I would often be overwhelmed with a feeling that is indescribable.

Sometimes I have cried out in agony for relief.

It was my spirit and the Holy Spirit in intercession for that unsaved congregation that I would meet at the evening hour.

After a while I learned what these depression periods meant.

But I wish to call your attention especially to Paul's prayers for the Church.

The first one is in Eph. 1:15,16: "For this cause I also, having heard of the faith in the Lord Jesus which is among you, and the love which ye show toward all the saints, cease not to give thanks for you, making mention of you in my prayers."

And here is a remarkable intercession for you and me. I am going to use the second person singular as Conybeare suggests: "That the God of my Lord Jesus Christ, the Father of glory, may give unto you a spirit of wisdom and revelation in the knowledge of him, having the eyes of your heart enlightened, that you may know what is the hope of his calling and what the riches of the glory of his inheritance in the saints."

Notice carefully now. He is praying that we may have a spirit of wisdom.

I don't know whether you have noticed it or not, but wisdom and knowledge are different.

Wisdom is the ability to use knowledge.

Wisdom doesn't come from the reasoning faculties, it comes from the human spirit. Whether it be natural wisdom of man outside of Christ, or whether it be God's wisdom that is given to the New Creation.

He is praying now that our spirits may have wisdom to grasp the riches of the work that God wrought in Christ Jesus for us.

It is Revelation Knowledge that was given to Paul.

Now we are to have wisdom to understand our share of Redemption's unveiling in that knowledge.

He says, "Having the eyes of our hearts illumined, that we may know the hope of his calling and the riches of the glory of the Father's inheritance in the saints," that is, in you and me.

If our hearts could grasp this, it would transform us.

If we could only realize what an inheritance the Father has in us, how priceless we are to Him.

We have our property insured in case of fire or theft.

We have our bodies insured in case of accident.

I wonder if the Father has His inheritance in us insured?

I wonder if He is as jealous over us as we are over our jewelry and our precious property? I am sure He is.

Some day we will make a discovery of how He has insured us.

Notice farther in the prayer. He wants us to know "the exceeding greatness of his ability on our behalf who believe."

He said, "it is according to the working of the strength of his might which he wrought in Christ, when he raised him from the dead."

My heart has been slow to grasp this.

When I knew in reality that the same ability that wrought in the dead body of Christ was at work within me, in my spirit, in my soul, in my body, then I knew that I was fortified.

I couldn't fail because I had become the instrument through which that Mighty One was working.

Then Rom. 8:11 cleared up: "But if the Spirit of him that raised up Jesus from the dead dwelleth in you, he that raised up Christ Jesus from the dead shall give life also to your mortal bodies through his Spirit that dwelleth in you."

The same power that wrought in Christ is in you and me.

That resurrection ability is in our bodies.

That means healing and strength and vitality for our present necessities in our daily walk.

But notice another thing he said: "And he made him to sit on his right hand in the heavenlies, far above all rule and authority and power and dominion, and every name that is named, not only in this age but also in that which is to come."

In Eph. 2:6 he says, "And raised us up with him, and made us to sit with him at his right hand," and we are sitting now far above all rule and authority.

That was Paul's prayer for us, or rather, it was the Spirit's prayer through Paul.

And now the Spirit goes farther and says, "He put all things in subjection under our feet."

We are the earth part of the Body of Christ.

The Executive is in the Heavens.

The office force is here on the earth; we are a part of that.

We must know that the ability God wrought in Christ when He raised Him from the dead is ours.

Here is another tremendous fact that we have almost utterly forgotten, "That He put all things in subjection under His feet and He gave Christ to be head over all things for the benefit of the Church."

We must not forget that Satan is defeated; that we were with Christ in that great Substitution of which we became a part; that we conquered the adversary with Him; when He arose from the dead, we were raised together with Him; and when He was enthroned at the right hand of the Father, we were enthroned with Him.

He is praying that we may know this, that we may enter into the fulness of it.

That prayer must be answered.

I am asking now that this prayer should be answered for each one of you who read this book.

"He has given Jesus to be head over all things for the benefit of the Church."

Then the "over all things" includes everything that can touch your life and mine. They are all subject to the Head–Christ; and they are subject to us – the Body of Christ.

For in that next verse He says, "Which is his body, the fulness of him that filleth all things."

The Body is the fulness of Him. The Body is the completeness of Him, and the Ability of the Body should dominate all things around it.

Our feeble intellects can't grasp this, but our spirits can revel in it.

For our spirits are filled with His fulness, the fulness of His Love, the fulness of His Grace, the fulness of His Wisdom, the fulness of His Ability to bless and help men.

His next prayer is in Eph. 3:14-21: "For this cause I bow my knees unto the Father, from whom every family in heaven and on earth is named."

Now notice the prayer: "That he would grant you, according to the riches of his glory, that ye may be strengthened with ability through his Spirit in the inward man."

Strengthened with God's Ability.

It doesn't seem to me that we can ever be weak or failures again.

I don't know what all that means, nor do I know the limits of it, but I do know that it makes us more than conquerors in the midst of every perplexing condition.

It puts our heel upon the neck of our enemies, whether they be spiritual enemies or material; it makes us masters.

It strips us of our weakness and inability and clothes us with the Ability from on High.

He says, "That Christ may dwell in your hearts" – in my heart and in yours – "on the ground of faith; to the end that we may be rooted and grounded in love."

That is the Jesus kind of love – Agapa.

We are not only to be influenced by it, but we are to be rooted and grounded in it; established in Love.

I John 4:16, "And we know and have believed the love which God hath in our case. God is love; and he that abideth in love abideth in God, and God abideth in him."

I think a better rendering is this: "We have come to believe in the love that God has in our case."

I have come to believe that Love, this Jesus kind of Love, is better than reason, better than force, better than philosophy of man, better than anything that man can devise.

Man's knowledge can't equal it.

I have come to believe that Love's way is the best way, and that the way of Love is the way to walk.

When I know that God is Love, then the way of God is best.

If I believe in Love, I believe in the Author of Love.

I do believe in Love.

I believe that His Love way is best for me; is best for you.

It is the end of strife for ourselves, the end of bitterness and hatred and jealousy.

It is the beginning of Christ dominating our lives in our earth walk.

To be rooted and grounded in love is the choicest experience that can ever come to the human heart.

"And then we will be strong to grasp with all the saints, what is the breadth and length and height and depth of His grace and of His Love."

We will come to know the love of Christ personally, so we will say as Paul did, "He loved me and He gave Himself up for me."

His Redemption will be a personal thing.

He did it for me.

It will be as though no other person lived; that I was the one for whom He died.

But you know the next sentence says, "And to know the love of Christ which passeth knowledge, that I may be filled with all the fulness of God."

That was His prayer for me.

That was his prayer for you.

That prayer can't go unanswered.

You remember how he groaned in Col. 1:28, "that I may present every man perfect in Christ."

That was the Spirit's passion in Paul.

God help me to have the same passion.

That eliminates selfishness utterly, doesn't it?

That is a new self, a self born of God, a self that has no dream but God's dream, no ambition but His ambition.

But hear the closing of that prayer: "Now unto him that is able to do exceeding abundantly above all that we ask or think."

You see, we swing out of the orbit of sense knowledge, out of the limitations of sense reason, into the realm of the supernatural.

We are living now in the realm of Grace, the realm of God.

He says that "it is above all that we can ask or think, according to the ability that worketh in us."

We have been slow to grasp this, but this is a picture of His Grace.

This is an illustration of the Father's dream for us.

This illustrates the prayer life of Paul.

It is better than any rules or regulations that man can make in regard to a prayer life.

When you and I realize this prayer was for us, we become anxious that it be answered in us.

That lets Him loose in us to work His own will and His own pleasure in and through us for His glory.

Chapter V

CHRIST IN THE LIGHT OF THE PAULINE REVELATION

HIS is an unveiling of what we are before the Father, and how the Father looks upon us in Christ.

John 16:28: "I came out from the Father, and am come into the world: again, I leave the world, and go unto the Father."

You remember Jesus said in John 3:3-5, "Except one be born from above, he cannot see the kingdom of God."

The believer is born of God. He comes out of the very womb of God.

"Whosoever is born of God overcometh the world."

"For in one Spirit were we all immersed into one body, and were all made to drink of one Spirit." (I Cor. 12:13).

Just as truly as Jesus came out from the Father, so we have come out from God through the energy of the Spirit. We are born of God.

In I John 4:4 we read, "Ye are of God my little children."

We are a part of the very Life of God.

God's very Nature has been poured into our spirits, for we are of God.

Now we can understand Jesus' confession. It staggered the Jews. It startled the disciples.

"I came out from the Father; I came into the world: again, I leave the world and go back to my Father."

Just as truly as we came out from the Father in our New Birth, when we leave our bodies, we go back to our Father.

In John 8:23 Jesus said, "Ye are from beneath; I am from above."

Jesus was ever conscious of His heavenly origin and of His heavenly relationship.

Nothing would help us so much as to be aware that we do not belong to the earth. We are on the earth but we are not of it. Our citizenship is in heaven.

We are no longer a part of this Satan-ruled world. We are born from above.

We have the Nature and the Life of the Father. We are in Christ.

Believers are in danger of being attracted to earthly things, such as money and the pleasures of life.

If we could know we are not of the earth, as we know we are men or women, and know that our highest joy is to be found alone in Christ, it would make a great difference in our earth walk.

In Matt. 12:42 Jesus said, "A greater than Solomon is here." He dared to confess what He actually was.

He dared to tell that generation that looked on Him with suspicion and jealousy and hatred, who He was. "A greater than Solomon is here."

I wonder if we have realized who we are? I wonder if we ever considered that we belong to another race?

2 Cor. 5:17 "Wherefore, if any man is in Christ, he is a new creation (a new species); the old things that belong to the earth walk are passed away, and behold all things are become new; but all these things are of God, who reconciled us unto himself."

We haven't realized that the least in the kingdom of God is greater than Solomon. He was but a servant. His vast wisdom was given to him.

We are the sons of God and Jesus has been made unto us Wisdom.

Solomon was but a natural man who lived in the realm of the senses. He had no conception of this Divine Life that has been given to us.

But we don't think of that.

We have not yet realized our position in Christ; our position in the Family.

We are the very Sons and Daughters of God Almighty. Solomon was but a son of David.

John 8:12 is perhaps one of the greatest sentences that ever fell from the lips of the Master, if we dared to put one Scripture over against another.

"I am the light of the world. He that followeth me shall not walk in the darkness, but shall have the Light of Life."

Jesus dared to say that He represented a new order, a new type of man, that in Him was the Light of Life; that is, the Wisdom that comes from Eternal Life.

The people who follow Him, walk in His footsteps and obey His word, should never be caught in the realm of darkness where they cannot see.

Col. 1:13 says, "Who delivered us out of the authority of darkness, and translated us into the kingdom of the Son of his love."

You see, we have been taken out of the realm of darkness where men walk by the senses.

We have been translated into the kingdom of the Son of His Love, or in other words, into the very Family of God.

We have become partakers of His Divine Nature. The same Life that was in the Son of God is in us. The same Light that He had is in us.

Now we can understand 2 Cor. 6:14: "Be not unequally yoked with unbelievers: for what fellowship have righteousness and iniquity? or what communion hath light with darkness?"

In Phil. 2:15 Paul tells us, "We are seen as lights in the world." We are holding forth as a lamp, the Word of Life.

We are the light of the world. We have taken Jesus' place.

His Life in us is the source of Light.

Light means Wisdom and ability to do things, and the Greater One has not only imparted to us His own Nature, but He has actually come into us and lives in us – has become a part of us.

So when Jesus said, "I am the light of the world," it placed tremendous responsibility upon those who follow in His steps.

If we are partakers of His Life, then we have that Light and John 1:4 must ever challenge us: "In him was life; and the Life was the light of men."

We have that Life.

With that Life has come the Light, and we must walk in the light as He is in the light.

To step out of that Light means to step into darkness, which means broken fellowship. It means to step out of the realm of Love, for that light is really Love shining out through us, in our conduct, in our words.

The new kind of Love and the new kind of Light which Jesus brought are the very Nature of the Father.

When we step out of Love we step out of Light, out of fellowship with Heaven.

If we walk in the Light as He is in the light, we have fellowship not only with the Father, but with one another. But when we are drawn aside for a moment by the adversary, we step into darkness.

I John 2:9-11, "He that saith he is in the light and hateth his brother, is in the darkness even until now.

"He that loveth his brother abideth in the light, and there is no occasion of stumbling in him.

"But he that hateth his brother is in the darkness, and walketh in the darkness, and knoweth not whither he goeth, because the darkness hath blinded his eyes."

His spirit is in darkness. Sense knowledge cannot light the path now.

We have taken the Master's place as lights in the world.

Just as Paul says, "Follow me as I follow Christ," so every one of us are lights in the world, and we are saying to the world, "Follow me as I follow Christ."

When we step out of light into darkness we spread confusion around us and folks know not what to do.

We should always remember what we are in Christ.

We should remember we are the lights of the world, and those that follow us must not be led into darkness.

John 14:6 has not only been a challenge, but has been a thrilling joy. Jesus said, "I am the way, the truth, and the life; no man cometh unto the Father, but by me."

What a confession that was!

When the Master said, "I am the Way," the Spirit at once began to bring to my mind excerpts from the 9th Chapter of Acts, of Paul going to Damascus to see if he could find any that were in the Way, whether men or women, so he could bring them to Jerusalem.

Christianity was the Way.

"But some were hardened and disobedient, speaking evil of The Way." (Acts 19:9).

What did they mean by calling Christianity The Way?

Back yonder in the Garden, Adam lost the Way, the Way into the Father's presence, the Way into the Father's heart.

He left the place of light and glory and went out into the world without light.

All down through human history men have been groping for the lost Way, the Way back into fellowship with the Father; back into that Edenic condition where condemnation would not rule as a Master over the heart.

When Jesus said, "I am the Way," He meant He was the Way to the Father's heart – the Way of Life.

Then I saw that everyone of us is a light, a sign-board pointing to the Way.

Now notice carefully what it means to you. You are taking the Master's place; you are the Way, and if your life is not in tune with the Master, and you are not living the Word, you may be pointing the wrong way.

He not only said, "I am the Way," but He said, "I am the Truth," or, "I am the Reality."

When I saw that word translated Reality, it gripped me.

Jesus is the answer of the age-old cry of the human spirit for Reality.

One translation of Rom. 1:25 reads, "For they exchange the reality of God for the unreal."

Satan is the God of vanity. The major pleasures of the Senses of natural man have no actual reality in them.

There is no reality in the moving pictures, in the dance hall, in gambling, or in drinking.

There is nothing in them that the spirit of man can feed upon.

Satan has not given to man one thing that has in it any permanent value.

The pleasures of the Senses perish with the using.

When Jesus said, "I am the Way, the Reality, and the Life," He was pointing to something that is different.

In John 16:13 Jesus said, "When he, the Spirit of Reality, is come, he will guide you into all Reality."

Jesus is the Way into the thing that the heart has craved through the ages – Reality.

It is a strangely realistic truth that no one who has ever actually found Eternal Life, has ever turned to any other religion.

The metaphysical religions that are born of the senses have no appeal for the man who has found Reality.

The human heart can find no Reality outside of the man Jesus.

The New Creation is real.

Our fellowship with the Father is real.

The Word is a real message to the spirit of the New Creation.

We walk in the light of Reality.

Jesus said: "I am the Way, the Reality, and the Life."

The Greek word here for Life is "Zoe." That is the new kind of Life Jesus brought to the world.

"I am come that ye might have life and have it in abundance."

What is Life? It is the Nature of the Father.

In that Nature of the Father is all Wisdom, all Ability, all Love.

John 6:47: "He that believeth hath Eternal Life."

Believing is actual possession, so the believer is a possessor of this the greatest gift ever given to man – Eternal Life.

John 1:4 "In him was Life, and that life is the light of men."

How little we have appreciated the fact that Eternal Life in man has given to us all the creative ability manifested in this mechanical age.

No heathen nation ever had any inventors or creators until Eternal Life came to them.

When we boast of Anglo-Saxon superiority, it is simply the superiority of Eternal Life over natural life.

There are two words translated Life in the New Testament: "Zoe"– the Nature of the Father that Jesus brought, and gives to man in the New Creation; and "Psuche" – the natural human life.

"Psuche" has never produced any great literature; has never given to man anything that was of any real value.

Let this become clear in our minds, that "Zoe," this new kind of Life, is the Nature of the Father, and the Father is Love.

So when this new kind of Life comes into a man, it drives out the old nature and the New Nature takes possession.

It is just like Israel moving into the promised land, driving out the inhabitants, and taking over the country for themselves.

Eternal Life has taken us over.

It has captivated our reasoning faculties, illuminating them, making them the slave of this New Order, so that wherever a man who has Eternal Life goes you see the marks of it.

He is a New Creation man. He belongs to the New Order of things.

He has a new kind of Love – Agapa – and that Love makes a home in which it is safe for babies to be born.

The other kind of love is the Greek word "Phileo," the love which springs from the natural human heart.

It has never made a home in a heathen country.

It is the parent of all our divorces and broken homes.

Where a man and woman have "Agapa," the new kind of Love that springs out of this new kind of Life, there is never a divorce.

This is the greatest thing in the world.

The believer is the sign-board pointing toward Jesus – the Way, the Truth, and the Life, and we must be bold in our confession that we are in the Way; that we have the Reality and are enjoying the fullness of this marvelous Life.

Jesus made another confession. "I am the Good Shepherd." The Good Shepherd lays down his life for the sheep." (John 10:11)

What a beautiful confession, so full of suggestion – the Shepherd.

It brings before the heart the 23rd Psalm: "Jehovah is my shepherd; I do not want. He causeth me to lie down in green pastures, and he leadeth me beside the waters of gentle stillness"; he restores my thinking processes so I can think God's thoughts.

He is the caretaker, the bread-provider, the shield and the protector of His people.

His ministry is guiding and leading us into the real pastures where the heart learns to feed.

Can you see what this means to you?

The moment we receive Eternal Life, that moment we become under-shepherds of the flock: we become leaders and teachers of this New Order, this new Life.

We are the protectors of the lambs from the adversary that would destroy them.

What a ministry of Love that shepherd has! What a life of Love caring for them, watching over them, feeding them, pointing the way to the Water of Life, and leading them into the quiet place under the shadow of the great Rock in this weary land.

We ought to make confession of our shepherd responsibility and our ability to guide men.

I was amazed when I found the Greek word translated power meant ability, and that Jesus wanted the disciples to tarry in Jerusalem until they had received ability – the Father's ability that Jesus had been manifesting among men.

Now we, the under-shepherds, have His ability. We are partakers of that ability.

He is made unto us Wisdom so we may know where to lead the sheep and what to feed them.

The greatest concern I have ever had regarding my ministry, was ability to rightly divide the Word so I could give men the food, the Bread of the Almighty.

I have wanted to be a Faith Builder. I wanted to lead men out of the wilderness of sense knowledge into the highlands of our privileges in Christ, which is a Shepherd's responsibility.

Here is another confession of Jesus that has a Pauline ring to it: "The words that I speak unto you are Spirit and are life" (John 6:63).

How few of us have realized the power of words. Jesus knew.

Jesus' words healed the sick, fed the multitudes, hushed the sea, raised the dead.

Not only that, but they stirred such malignity and hatred in the hearts of the leaders of Israel that they finally nailed Him to the cross, just because of the words that He had spoken.

Paul makes us see it with a vividness that thrills. "By faith we understand that the worlds have been framed by the Word of God, so that what is seen hath not been made out of things which appear" (Heb. 11 :3).

God created the Universe with Words.

You remember those three wonderful words, "Let there be." Eight or nine times those words are recorded in the first Chapter of Genesis.

God brought everything that is in the Universe into being with words.

But the Spirit climaxes it in John 1:1-3: "In the beginning was the Word, and the Word was with God, and the Word was God. The same was in the beginning with God. All things were made through him; and without him was not anything made that hath been made."

He took man's words and filled them with Himself.

He made man's words creative things.

He filled man's words with the very genius of Love.

His words dominated.

He indwelt words and made them work for Him.

He counted the things that were not as though they were, and they leaped into being.

Words create.

Then in Heb. 1:3, words dominated the things that words had created: "Who being the effulgence of his glory, and the very image of his substance, and upholding all things by the word of his power, when he made purification of sins, sat down on the right hand of the Majesty on high."

He had brought the world into being with His Word. Now that vast Universe is sustained and governed by His Word.

Oh, my heart craves for the hour to come when we will begin to appreciate what words can accomplish.

All the business the world ever did was with words.

With words we make love.

With words we crush hearts.

With words – God-filled words – we build faith into the lives of men.

With words that are filled with sense knowledge, we destroy the faith of men.

Sense knowledge has no other means but words, and so our universities are filled with words, oftentimes destructive words, demoralizing words.

Our high schools are destroying the faith of our nation with false teaching – all with words.

34

There is nothing holy any longer.

An ideology borne of sense knowledge is dominating our nation, and unless the Word of God gains the ascendency again, all the ideals of our Republic will go, and a new type of despotism that is destructive to Christianity will take its place.

Men without God have used the inventions that God has given to the New Creation to destroy all God has wrought through the Church since the Lutheran Reformation.

When Jesus said, "The words that I speak unto you they are spirit and they are life," He was lifting the curtain and letting us see the realities.

Think of it! "The words that I speak," have in them the power and energy and Creative Ability of God.

"The words that I speak unto you," are life-giving words, love-building words, faith-creating words.

Now what is our confession?

Our confession is that we are the products of His words, that His words have given to our spirits the very Nature of the Father, and that the law that governs this new Life is the Law of the New Covenant.

"A new commandment give I unto you that ye love one another, even as I have loved you" (John 13:34).

This new Law that grows out of the Love Nature of the Father is the Law that governs us.

We are walking in the light of this New Law, this Creative, dominating Law, this victorious Law of Love.

What a confession we have to make. God help us to hold fast to it.

In John 14:9 Jesus says, "He that hath seen me hath seen the Father."

That almost takes one's breath away.

Jesus said, "Have I been so long a time with you and you do not know what I am? I am God manifest in the flesh."

"You have been living and walking with God.

"You have seen Him heal the sick and raise the dead.

"You have seen Him feed the multitudes through me.

"You have felt His Love Nature in my voice and in my words, and so I say to you today, 'He that hath seen me hath seen the Father.'

"You need never say again, 'Show us the Father,' for He is with you."

What a confession that was! How it has lingered in the very atmosphere through the ages!

Then one day I caught a glimpse of the Revelation of the New Creation in the Pauline Epistles, and I saw we were actually taking Jesus' place; that we had the same Life in us Jesus had, and the same Nature of the Father has been imparted to us.

With that Nature have come all the attributes that made Jesus so beautiful to the world and made Him stand out as the most unusual character the ages have ever seen.

Every attribute in Jesus that made Him beautiful is in the New Creation.

We have the same Life that dominated Him – that Love Nature.

We have the same kind of Love He had.

He is made unto us Wisdom from God.

He is made unto us Redemption from God.

He is made unto us Sanctification from God.

He is made unto us Righteousness from God.

Those four attributes of the very Nature of the Father were manifest in Jesus.

Redemption from the hand of the adversary had not yet been accomplished when Jesus walked the earth, but it was manifested in Him. He was the Master of demons.

Sanctification was revealed in Him in His utter separation from the world that surrounded Him.

Righteousness, the ability to stand in the Father's presence without the sense of inferiority, the ability to stand in the presence of Satan as a master – all those gracious manifestations of the Divine Life were seen in Him.

As I read John 14:6-10, my whole being seems to open up toward Him and my heart cries, "Lord, make this real by thy Grace in my life so men who see me will see you; so I can say, perhaps not in words, 'He that hath seen me hath seen the Master.' "

What a confession Jesus made to the world, and what a confession we have the privilege of making today.

Jesus said "I am the vine, ye are the branches."

I would that my heart could understand it; that the heart could grasp the reality of our union with Him, of our unusual ability to feed upon the very Nature and Life of God in Christ.

You see, no branch can be closer to the vine than another branch.

Every branch has the same union with the vine for its individual ministry of fruit bearing.

When He said, "I am the vine, ye are the branches," it brought us into the fullest union with Deity.

We are actually partakers of the Divine Nature.

The very life and substance of Deity pours out of the vine into the branch.

Then He said in that great prayer in the 17th Chapter of John, "And the glory which thou hast given me, I have given unto them; that they may be one, even as we are one; I in them, and thou in me, that they may be perfected into one."

Why? "That the world may know that thou hast sent me, and lovest them even as thou lovest me."

That is the Vine Life.

That is where the branch is glorified and the fruitage becomes like the fruitage of Jesus in His earth walk.

We can understand now what He meant when He said, "Greater works than these shall ye do; because I go unto My Father." (John 4:12)

Jesus was limited to physical things.

He could heal the sick, feed the multitudes, raise the dead, and turn water into wine, but He could not Recreate anyone.

He could not give anyone Eternal Life because it was not available until after He had put sin away, until He had satisfied the claims of justice, conquered Satan, arose from the dead, carried His blood into the heavenly Holy of Holies, and sat down at the right hand of the Majesty on High.

Chapter VI

WHAT THE RESURRECTION GIVES US

ERE are some of the riches of this blessed Truth gleaned from the Pauline Epistles.

What does His Resurrection mean to the Christian in his daily life?

John 19:31-37 tells us of His death, of the spear-thrust in His side, and of blood and water pouring out of that great gaping wound.

It is told in the plainest language that He died of a ruptured heart.

The blood flowed through the rupture in His heart into the sack that holds the heart, and as the body grew cold, the blood had separated and the white serum had settled to the bottom.

The red corpuscles had risen to the top and coagulated, and when that Roman spear pierced it, the white serum gushed out.

Then followed clots of the coagulated blood rolling down His side to the ground. Jesus was dead.

John 19:38-40, "And after these things Joseph of Arimathaea, being a disciple of Jesus, but secretly for fear of the Jews, asked of Pilate that he might take away the body of Jesus: and Pilate gave him leave. He came therefore, and took away His body.

"And there came also Nicodemus, he who at the first came to him by night, bringing a mixture of myrrh and aloes, about a hundred pounds. So they took the body of Jesus, and bound it in linen cloths with the spices, as the custom of the Jews is to bury."

Here is a drama worthy of inspiration.

Joseph and Nicodemus showed their friendship openly after His death.

"Now in the place where he was crucified there was a garden; and in the garden a new tomb wherein was never man yet laid. There then because of the Jews' Preparation (for the tomb was nigh at hand) they laid Jesus." (Verses 41-42.)

John 20:1-10, gives us a picture of His Resurrection. "Now on the first day of the week cometh Mary Magdalene early, while it was yet dark, unto the tomb, and seeth the stone taken away from the tomb.

"She runneth therefore, and cometh to Simon Peter, and to the other disciple whom Jesus loved, and saith unto them, They have taken away the Lord out of the tomb, and we know not where they have laid him.

"Peter therefore went forth, and the other disciple, and they went toward the tomb.

"And they ran both together: and the other disciple outran Peter, and came first to the tomb; and stooping and looking in, he seeth the linen cloths lying; yet entered he not in.

"Simon Peter therefore also cometh, following him, and entered into the tomb; and he beholdeth the linen cloths lying, and the napkin, that was upon his head, not lying with the linen cloths, but rolled up in a place by itself.

"Then entered in therefore the other disciple also, who came first to the tomb, and he saw, and believed.

"For as yet they knew not the scripture, that he must rise again from the dead.

"So the disciples went away again unto their own home."

What a shock it must have been to Mary.

She had come to the sepulchre to finish the embalming and saw the stone rolled away.

She never stopped to look in but turned and ran back to the room where Peter and John were stopping.

Bursting in upon them she cried, "They have taken away my Lord, and I know not where they have laid him."

Who had dared to desecrate the tomb?

No people among all the nations paid such reverence to the dead as the Hebrew Nation.

The Romans had stripped Him; they had scourged Him; they had nailed Him to the cross, with a mock crown on His Head. That wasn't enough.

Had they dared to desecrate the grave?

Peter and John would not wait; they both started toward the tomb.

John outran Peter and arrived there first.

Stooping down, he looked into the tomb and was staggered at what he saw.

Peter came. He hadn't the fine feelings that actuated John. He just bowed his head and stepped into the sepulchre and John followed him.

Notice the language: "And he beholdeth the linen cloths lying, and the napkin that was upon his head not lying with the linen cloths, but laid in a place by itself."

When Jesus came out of the grave clothes there was no hurry. He picked up the napkin that had been upon His face, folded it up and laid it in a niche in the tomb.

There is something about that act of the Master that reaches deep into my spirit-consciousness.

He doesn't act like a man, does he?

Only God would act like that in an hour of such triumph.

"Then entered therefore that other disciple also who came first to the tomb, and he saw and believed."

What did John see in the sepulchre that made him believe that Jesus was resurrected?

"Up to this time they knew not the scripture that he must rise again from the dead."

You understand, Jesus' body had been embalmed as the custom of the Jews was to bury.

Nearly every rich family had a slave who understood embalming.

They had one hundred pounds of a mixture composed of myrrh and aloes and a bundle of linen cloths.

They cut the linen up into strips, smeared it with this mixture as you would a bandage to wrap around a wounded finger, and then wrapped the body of Jesus.

Every finger was wrapped separately and then the hands and arms, until the whole body was wrapped as an Egyptian mummy. When it was finished, they took the embalmed body and put it into the sepulchre, and it was sealed by Roman authority.

Notice, the body of Jesus likely weighed 180 to 200 pounds in his health. He would shrink about twenty pounds in the crucifixion.

There was a hundred pound weight of myrrh and aloes, besides the linen cloths they used in embalming. Then the body would weigh about 280 pounds.

When they had finished the embalming, His body was completely encased except for His face.

If Jesus had not died of a ruptured heart and the spear thrust, He certainly would have died in the three days and three nights of embalming.

No one could have lived thru that.

The embalming cloth had grown hard and stiff in that dry cell in the seventy-two hours He was there.

The cloth had not been rent or torn. He had come out of the grave clothes through the narrow aperture where His face had been.

What do you think Peter and John did?

No sooner had they left the sepulchre, than they rushed through the streets crying, "He is risen! He is risen!"

Their hearts were so overcharged with emotion they couldn't resist proclaiming the fact.

The tremendous stir His resurrection made in the city, three thousand men that accepted Christ on the Day of Pentecost, all prove the historic fact, the absolute certainty of His resurrection.

The whole Jewish nation knew it. They were shaken to the foundation.

I Cor. 15:1-8 declares that five hundred people saw Him at His ascension.

The early Church did not try to prove that Jesus arose from the dead. It was a self-evident fact.

No one ever questioned it in Jerusalem.

They were there when it happened.

They saw the tomb and the empty grave clothes.

Tens of thousands of Jews went to that empty sepulchre, stood there smiting their breasts and rending their garments.

They knew Jesus had risen.

Now what does it mean to us today?

Rev. 1:17, 18, hear the Resurrected Master speaking now: "And when I saw him, I fell at his feet as one dead. And he laid his right hand upon me, saying, Fear not; I am the first and the last, and the Living one; and I was dead, and behold, I am alive forevermore, and I have the keys of death and of Hades."

Satan had been conquered.

What a thrill went through the whole spirit world when Jesus came from the dark regions, a Master, holding aloft in His hand the keys of death and of hell.

He had stripped that foul spirit of his authority.

He had left him defeated before his own cohorts.

There was a spiritual earthquake in the region of the damned.

Heb. 2:14 tells us, "Since then the children are sharers in flesh and blood, he also himself in like manner partook of the same; that through death he might bring to nought him that had the authority of death, that is, the devil."

Rotherham translates it "that he might paralyze the death-dealing authority of the devil." Either translation is clear enough.

Before Jesus arose from the dead, He had conquered Satan and stripped him of the authority of which he had robbed man in the Garden.

The story of the triumph of Satan's defeat wouldn't be fully described unless we gave you Col. 2:15: "Having despoiled the principalities and the powers, he made a show of them openly, triumphing over them in it."

The margin reads, "Having put off from himself the principalities and the powers."

You see, Jesus was held down there and only God knows what He suffered until He had satisfied the claims of justice, had been made Righteous, and made a New Creation.

Then Satan's dominion over Him ended. He hurled back the hosts of hell.

He crushed their death-dealing ability.

He stripped Satan of his authority and left him paralyzed and broken. Then He arose from the dead and shouted, "All hail," for Redemption morn had come!

Redemption was a fact. Satan was defeated.

Now we can quote Col. 1:13 once more. I want you to become familiar with this scripture. I want you to know it as you know two and two are four.

"Who delivered us out of the authority of darkness, and translated us into the kingdom of the Son of his love; in whom we have our redemption, the remission of our trespasses."

That was the greatest moment in human history.

That was a moment that will be remembered through all eternity, when Jesus stood before the wondering disciples and shouted, "All hail!"

Angels must have wept before the throne.

The great Father God – what could it have meant to Him?

Humanity, the hope of His Love and the reason for all Creation, was Redeemed; the claims of Justice were satisfied.

The Throne could never be assailed. God had legally redeemed man.

All the ages of eternity will remember the heroic battle that Jesus wrought in order to prove to humanity that God was just and He could on legal grounds justify the ungodly, because His only Begotten Son had redeemed them with His own blood.

Now God can on legal grounds give to man Eternal Life.

John 5:24 and 6:47 can become a part of human experience. "He that heareth my word, and believeth him that sent me, hath eternal life, and cometh not into judgment, but hath passed out of death into life."

I wonder if your heart takes this in?

There will be no Judgment for us like there was for the Master;

there will be no cross and no crown of thorns.

There will be no suffering in hell for the man who takes Jesus Christ as his Savior—and it is so easy to take Him.

Hear this Scripture: John 6:47, "He that believeth hath eternal life," or he that acts upon the Word that God has spoken, has Eternal Life the moment that he acts.

The man outside of Christ cannot confess the Lordship of Jesus and declare that he knows Christ died for his sins and arose when He was Justified, without receiving the Nature and Life of God.

You ask, what is the greatest miracle of all the miracles connected with Redemption?

It is not the Resurrection of the Lord Jesus, because the Father and the Son were working together in that.

But the greatest miracle happens when a man receives Eternal Life, when a child of the devil becomes a Child of God.

Notice again: When a man who is spiritually dead passes out of the realm of Satan into the realm of Life (into the Kingdom of the Son of God's Love) that is the miracle of miracles.

To the sense knowledge man, the Resurrection is the greatest miracle, because that is something the senses can register.

But the New Birth is an unseen miracle. It is in the Spirit Realm.

Man's soul or reasoning faculties cannot be Born Again. They cannot receive the Nature of God independent of his spirit.

His spirit is the part of him that is Recreated.

2 Cor. 5:17-21 had become a Reality the moment Jesus carried His blood into the Holy of Holies and sat down at the right hand of the Father.

Now a man can accept Christ and know that the moment he does, he becomes a New Creation.

The old things of his life have passed away, and behold all are become new; and all these things are of God, who has reconciled that man to Himself through Jesus Christ.

What a miracle the New Creation is!

Think of taking a man out of the very dregs of our modern civilization and Recreating him in a single moment from a convict to a Son of God.

And not only that, but notice that 21st verse. Here God whispers, "Him who knew no sin, I made to become sin, that I might make you my righteousness in Christ."

That is the Father speaking, and the moment you accept Christ as your Savior and confess Him as your Lord, that moment you become the Righteousness of God in Christ.

We could stop here, for this is enough to thrill the ages, but we haven't reached the climax of Redemption yet.

I Cor. 1:9, "God is faithful, through whom ye were called into the fellowship of his Son Jesus Christ our Lord."

It took me a good while before I could adjust my heart to the reality of that statement, that the great Eternal Father God, the Creator of the Universe, should call me, should call you to fellowship with His Son, to become Identified with that Son, to become one with that Son.

Here are a beautiful father and mother. They have a lovely boy, and oh, how careful they have been in his upbringing. Could you think of them going down into the slums and finding a nondescript child to be his associate, to fellowship with that boy? No.

But here is the miracle.

The Father knows when a man accepts His Son as his Savior, and confesses His Lordship, that moment He will give that man something that will make him absolutely a New Creation.

He will be in the same class with Jesus.

He will be an actual Child of God.

The old spiritual nature that links him with Satan has ceased being, and a New Nature, God's own Nature, is imparted to him.

Now he is as really the Father's Son as was Jesus in His earth walk, and he is as Righteous as the First Begotten, because that First Begotten is his Righteousness.

You may talk about miraculous things, but I declare to you, this New Creation miracle outstrips everything in all Creation.

Taking a child of the devil with his hands wet with the blood of his brother, and changing that man's nature! No sir! Giving that man a New Nature, destroying the old nature; giving him the position of a Son; giving him the rights and privileges of a Son; giving him the very place of a Son in the Father's heart and Family – here is Grace; here is Love let loose.

This is a picture of Paul.

This is the climax. Now you are ready to turn to 2 Cor. 2:14-16: "But thanks be unto God, who always leadeth us in triumph in Christ, and maketh manifest through us the fragrance of his knowledge in every place."

Now note this: "For we are a sweet fragrance of Christ unto God, in them that are saved, and in them that are perishing; to the one a savor from death unto death; to the other a savor from life unto life. And who is sufficient for these things?"

And then hear this cry: "For we are not as the many, corrupting the word of God: but we have been made sufficient to fulfil this ministry."

But I want you to notice a little sentence taken from the Conybeare Translation commenting on those verses.

"But thanks be to God, who leads me on from place to place in the train of his triumph, to celebrate his victory over the enemies of Christ; and by me sends forth knowledge of Him, a steam of fragrant incense, throughout the world. For Christ's is the fragrance which I offer up to God."

The metaphor is taken from the triumphal procession of a victorious general. God is celebrating His triumph over His enemies; Paul (who had been so great an opponent of the Gospel) is a captive following in the train of the triumphal procession, yet (at the same time, by a characteristic change of metaphor) an incense-bearer, scattering incense (which was always done on these occasions) as the procession moves on.

Some of the conquered enemies were put to death when the procession reached the Capitol; to them the smell of the incense was 'an odor of death unto death'; to the rest who were spared, 'an odor of life unto life.'

The heart can hardly grasp the significance of it.

We now reign as Masters and Kings.

Once more I want to give you Rom. 5:17 for it fits here perfectly. (Weymouth's Translation, 3d Ed.) "For if, through the transgression of one individual, Death made use of the one individual to seize the sovereignty, all the more shall those who receive God's overflowing grace and gift of righteousness reign as kings in Life through the one individual, Jesus Christ."

We are now reigning as kings in the realm of life.

We have become Masters. We are conquerors.

What does the Resurrection mean to us?

It means that He has taken us from slavery to the Throne.

We were defeated, conquered, and held in bondage.

We are set free, and in the name of Jesus we become the bondage-breakers for the rest of the human race.

He has made us Masters where fear held us in captivity.

CHAPTER VII

"IN WHOM WE HAVE"

ANY believers are afraid to say that they are in Christ and are afraid to act as though it is true.

The Father has declared in the Word what we are in Christ. We find believers seeking to obtain what love has already given them.

We ought to know what we are and what we have in Him.

First, what we have in Christ. Col. 1:13, "Who delivered us out of the power of darkness, and translated us into the kingdom of the Son of his love; in whom we have our redemption, the remission of our sins."

I shall use in this the first person singular as Conybeare suggests. Then it would read, "Who delivered me out of the authority of darkness, and translated me into the kingdom of the Son of his love; in whom I have my redemption and the remission of my sins."

Our Redemption is from the dominion of Satan, and when Christ arose from the dead and presented His own blood before the Supreme Court of the Universe, and it was accepted, our Redemption was a settled thing.

Then He sat down at the right hand of the Majesty on High.

When he sat down, Satan had been defeated. Everything that justice had demanded had been accomplished.

Now God has, a legal right to give man Eternal Life, but He had no right to give man Eternal Life until there had been a perfect Redemption.

So Rom. 3:21-26 is the Holy Spirit's exposition of this blessed Reality. "But now apart from the law a righteousness of God hath been unveiled, being witnessed by the law and the prophets."

You understand that man's basic need was Righteousness, the ability to stand in the Father's presence without the sense of guilt or inferiority, and so He declares that God has unveiled a new source of Righteousness, and that source of Righteousness is witnessed by the law and the prophets, "even the righteousness of God on the ground of faith in Jesus Christ."

And the strange thing is that it is based upon simple faith in Jesus, or in acting upon what God has said in regard to His Son.

In the 24th verse he says, "Being justified freely by his grace through the redemption that is in Christ Jesus."

You understand, He was delivered up on the account of our trespasses, and He was raised when we were justified. (Rom. 4:25).

Then he declares in the next verse, "Being therefore justified on the ground of faith, we have found peace with God through our Lord Jesus Christ."

Now we can understand that we were Justified freely by his Grace, through the Redemption God wrought in Christ, Whom He has set forth to be a sin substitute on the ground of Faith and His blood.

God did this to show His Righteousness because He had been passing over the sins of Israel for fifteen hundred years.

Now it is demanded that the penalty be paid.

Jesus met that penalty and paid or redeemed the promises that were each year made by the High Priest on the great Day of Atonement.

Jesus cashed all those promissory notes and brought Redemption to every man who had been blood-covered under the First Covenant.

I think we ought to read Heb. 9:12, "Nor yet with the blood of goats and calves, but with his own blood, entered in once for all into the holy place, having obtained eternal redemption."

I want you to note that this Redemption is an Eternal Redemption.

That when Christ carried His blood into the Holy of Holies, and the Supreme Court of the Universe accepted it, Redemption was a completed thing.

"For if the blood of goats and bulls, and the ashes of a heifer sprinkling them that have been defiled, sanctify unto the cleanness of the flesh: how much more shall the blood of Christ, who through the eternal Spirit offered himself without blemish unto God, cleanse your conscience from dead works to serve the living God?"

Did you notice that the blood of bulls and goats only cleanses the flesh?

The cleansing of the flesh means the senses; it did not cleanse the heart; it did not make man a New Creation.

Now notice the 15th verse: "And for this cause he is the mediator of a New Covenant, that a death having taken place for the redemption of the transgressions that were under the first covenant, they that have been called may receive the promise of the eternal inheritance."

Now you can understand what he meant in Rom. 3. He died for the sins of those living under the First Covenant that had been

47

covered by blood from year to year, that they might have their share in the inheritance and in this Redemption.

You see, the Redemption in Christ not only reached forward to us, but reached backward and redeemed every man under the First Covenant who had trusted in the blood of bulls and goats.

Heb. 9:26 now becomes clear to us: "But now once at the end of the ages hath he been manifested to put away sin by the sacrifice of himself."

He has dealt with the sin problem.

Now it is a sinner problem.

The sin problem is ended and the sinner has the legal right to Eternal Life, because God so loved him that He gave him His only Begotten Son.

Redemption then is a settled fact, and it is possible now for a man to receive Eternal Life on legal grounds.

2 Cor. 5:17, "Wherefore, if any man is in Christ, he is a new Creation: the old things are passed away, behold they are become new. But all things are of God, who reconciled us to himself through Christ."

Note very carefully that in this New Creation, the man who accepts Christ receives Eternal Life.

Spiritual death, the nature of the adversary, is driven out of him, stops being in him, and a New Nature is given to him. His spirit is Recreated.

His soul or mind will need to be renewed.

(We deal with this in another chapter.)

But the mind and spirit must be brought into fellowship with each other, and that can only be as the mind is renewed through the Word.

It is very important that the believer sees this fact.

In Rom. 6:5, "For if we have become united with him in the likeness of his death, we shall be also in the likeness of his resurrection; knowing this, that our old man was crucified with him."

Notice the tense here. Not *is* crucified with Him, but *was* crucified.

The same truth is brought out in Gal. 2:20. "I have been crucified with Christ." The old version reads, "I am crucified with Christ."

Our crucifixion and union with Christ on the cross belong to the legal side of the plan of redemption.

All that He did for us in His Redemptive work is based on legal grounds. (The legal is always in the past tense.)

48

He was delivered up on account of our trespasses.

He died for our sins.

He arose for our justification. This is all in the past tense.

Now notice Rom. 6:6: "For this we know, that our old self was crucified with Christ, in order that the slave of sin might be destroyed; so that we should no longer be in slavery to sin." (Centenary Translation).

We died with Christ. We were raised together with Him.

So the old man, the sin nature that was a partaker of spiritual death, died with Christ.

When we accept Jesus Christ as our Savior and confess Him as our Lord, we become a New Creation, and experimentally that old man stops being and the New Man in Christ takes his place.

This has been a hard problem for many people. They say, "How can that be true in the face of Paul's experience in the 7th of Romans?"

Rom. 7:7-24 is Paul's experience as a Jew under the Law. It is not the experience of a New Creation.

He said in the 14th verse, "For we know that the law is spiritual: but I am carnal, sold under sin."

The Law was fulfilled in Christ. Nobody is under the Law today.

It is true, the Jew didn't know that he died with Christ and that his old Law and the First Covenant all ceased to be in Christ.

He doesn't know it today, but it is the truth.

The Law was the Jews' school-master until Christ; not as some translators try to make us believe, that the Law is our school-master to lead us to Christ. The Greek text shows conclusively that the law was until Christ, and when Christ arose from the dead and sat down on the right hand of the Majesty on high, the Abrahamic Covenant and the Mosaic Law stopped functioning.

There is no one under the Mosaic Law today. They can't get under it.

They may attempt it as many are doing today, but it is only a farce.

We have a New Law that belongs to the New Covenant, of which Christ is the Head, and that New Law is to govern the New Creation in Christ Jesus.

So I John 5:12,13 becomes a blessed Reality. "He that hath the Son hath the life; He that hath not the Son of God hath not the life. These things have I written unto you, that ye may know that ye have eternal life, even unto you that believe on the name of the Son of God."

The believer has Eternal Life.

He has passed out of death into life; out of the realm of Satan into the realm of Christ.

Out of the realm of spiritual death where Satan reigns, into the realm of Eternal Life where Jesus Christ reigns.

Notice the first sentence in I John 4:4: "Ye are of God, my little children."

We are of God. That fits in perfectly with John 3, where Jesus said to Nicodemus, "Ye must be born from above. That which is born of the flesh is flesh; and that which is born of the Spirit is spirit. Marvel not that I said unto thee, Ye must be born from above."

The New Creation is born from above.

They came from, God.

This new Nature flowed out from the very heart of the Father into their spirits, when they crowned Jesus as Lord of their lives.

Eph. 1:3 "Blessed be the God and Father of our Lord Jesus Christ, who hath blessed us with every spiritual blessing in Christ."

When we accepted Jesus Christ as our Saviour, then Rom. 8:32 became an actual reality. "What then shall we say to these things? If God is for us, who is against us? He that spared not his own Son, but delivered him up for us all, how shall he not also with him freely give us all things."

In that other verse you will notice that He has blessed us with every spiritual blessing.

Everything that Christ wrought in His Redemptive work belongs to the New Creation.

You do not need to pray for it or seek for it, nor believe for it; it is yours.

Phil. 4:6-7 gives us just another angle of our inheritance in Christ. "In nothing be anxious; but in everything by prayer and supplication with thanksgiving let your requests be made known unto God."

Then a miracle happens: "The peace of God, which passeth all understanding, shall guard your hearts and your thoughts in Christ Jesus."

When we know what our Redemption means to the Father, and what He intended it should mean to us, then we pass out of the realm of worry and fear and doubt.

Phil. 4:11 (Twentieth Century Translation): "Not that I speak in respect of want, for I have learned in whatsoever state I am, therein to be independent of circumstances."

Why can we be independent of circumstances? Because the 13th verse says, "I can do all things in him that strengtheneth me."

You see, this Redemption in the mind of the Father means a New Creation.

It means Sonship with all its privileges.

It means that we have come into the Family and have Family rights and privileges now that nothing can interrupt as long as we walk in Love with Him.

The second fact is what we are in Christ.

It is necessary for us to review a little.

We are Redeemed. Satan's dominion over us is ended. He no longer reigns over us.

Not only are we Redeemed, but the moment we came into the Family of God we became Satan's master.

God has given to us a legal right to the use of Jesus' name, and Matt. 28:19 declares, "All authority has been given unto me in heaven and on earth. Go ye therefore, and make disciples (or students) of all nations...and lo, I am with you always, even unto the end of the age."

How is He with us? He is with us, in His name, in His Word, and in the person of the Holy Spirit.

In Mark 16:17 He said, "And these signs shall follow them that believe: in my name shall they cast out demons; they shall speak with new tongues; they shall take up serpents, and if they drink any deadly thing, it shall in no wise hurt them; they shall lay hands on the sick, and they shall recover."

And the 20th verse: "And they went forth, and preached everywhere, the Lord working with them, and confirming the word by the signs that followed."

You see, He has not left us at the mercy of an enemy.

The youngest babe in Christ has a legal right to the Name of Jesus.

Not only that, but he has a legal right to the Indwelling Presence of the Holy Spirit.

I can never tell you what that means to my heart.

I John 4:4, that last clause: "For greater is he that is in you than he that is in the world."

What will He do when He comes in? He will guide us into all Truth or Reality (John 16:13).

He will take the things of Jesus and unveil them to our hearts.

He will impart to us the very ability of God.

If you remember, before Jesus went away, He told his disciples to tarry in Jerusalem until they be endued with power from on high.

That word power means ability.

The Holy Spirit was going to come into them with Divine Ability and make them masters of circumstances, masters of situations, masters of nations.

So He can say, "Fear thou not, for I am with thee: be not dismayed; for I am thy God: I will strengthen thee; yea, I will help thee; yea, I will uphold thee with the right hand of my righteousness." (Isa. 41:10).

That belongs to us today. That is a picture of the New Creation.

Not only did He give us Eternal Life and the great mighty Holy Spirit to live in our bodies, but He has made us the Righteousness of God in Christ.

Jesus' life during His earth walk was amazing to men of sense knowledge.

Righteousness made Jesus absolute master of every situation – a master of all men because all men were sin-conscious. Jesus was not.

Shakespeare said, "Sin makes cowards of us all." He struck the tap-root of the sin problem.

When a man becomes a New Creation, he receives the same Righteousness that Jesus had.

Jesus becomes his Righteousness. (I Cor. 1 :30).

That Righteousness makes him a master of demons; makes him a master of circumstances.

He is not afraid of Satan, or anything Satan can do or has done.

The early Church lived the new Creation in Reality. They were the Righteousness of God in actual demonstration.

Not only did the early Christians have Righteousness given to them but they were made the Righteousness of God in Christ. When they received the Righteous Nature of the Father, that Nature made them Righteous.

When they received the Love Nature of the Father, it made them Sons of Love.

That is the reason they could suffer any kind of persecution and yet love the persecutor.

Jesus loved Judas and the man who drove the nails into His hands and feet.

Paul loved the men who beat him and stoned him.

Stephen, when he was dying, said, "Father, forgive them; they know not what they do."

That was a new kind of Love the world had never known.

God is Love.

The New Creation has the Love Nature of the Father.

There is another outstanding feature that we must not overlook.

We have known God as a Loving God, a just God, a Holy God, but we have never thought of Him as a Faith God.

That is an outstanding characteristic of God.

He created the Universe by Faith.

Everything that came into being at Creation, came into being by faith. All He did was to say, "Let there be" and things became.

God is a Faith God.

No doubt everyone reading this will look back at his early Christian life.

When he was first Born Again he was filled with love; he was filled with zeal that was born of faith.

Could he have had the right teaching, he would have walked into a life of Faith that would have shaken the community.

You see, we become partakers of the Faith and Nature of God.

That explains that passage in Rom. 12:3, "According as God hath dealt to each man a measure of faith."

Every man at the New Birth has a measure of Faith. That measure can be increased as he uses it.

But under the modern teaching, what faith was given to him in the New Birth is usually destroyed by sense knowledge teaching.

We must not omit Eph. 2:10: "For we are his workmanship, created in Christ Jesus for good works, which God afore prepared that we should walk in them."

If we could continually remember that we are God's New Creations, that He was the Author and Finisher of these New Creations, just as He is the Author and Finisher of Faith, then life would be victorious.

He gave birth to us in the birth throes of agony in His Substitutionary work. We are the product of that birth.

You see, we have become the Sons and Daughters of God.

We remember that Jesus is our example.

Jesus never tried to believe. He acted on the Word of His Father. He never sought Faith.

He said He did what His Father told Him to do.

We urge the unsaved to get something. We should urge them to act on the Word.

Jesus belongs to them. All they need to do is to confess His Lordship, and the moment they do they receive Eternal Life.

Believing is acting on the Word.

The believer is one who has acted on the Word.

The unbeliever is one who has not yet acted.

The one is a possesser; the other may be merely a seeker after something that he has not claimed as his own.

I want you to know in your heart that you are what He says you are.

He wants you to act it, to confess what He has done in you; what He has made you to be.

This will glorify Him and strengthen your Faith.

To deny what we are and to tell what Satan is doing in our bodies or minds, is denying what we are in Christ.

All things are possible now, for we are the children of God. We are united with Him.

Chapter VIII

THE LEGAL AND VITAL ASPECTS OF REDEMPTION

NTIL one becomes conscious of these two phases of revelation, there will be a haziness in his teaching and a lack of solidity in his thinking and living.

The legal side of Redemption is what God did for us in Christ. It is in the past.

Rom. 4:25 is a good illustration: "Who was delivered up for our trespasses, and was raised for our justification."

Here is another: I Cor. 15:3,4 "For I delivered unto you first of all that which also I received: that Christ died for our sins according to the scriptures; and that he was buried; and that he hath been raised on the third day according to the scriptures."

These two scriptures perfectly illustrate what God did for us in His Redemptive work.

The vital can be illustrated. Rom. 8:1: "There is therefore now no condemnation to them that are in Christ Jesus." Col. 1:14 "In whom we have our redemption, the remission of our sins."

The vital is what we really have now; what the Holy Spirit is doing in us today.

If one only had the legal side of the plan of Redemption, it would lead him into cold, dead formalism.

It would make doctrines out of Reality and sense knowledge would rule.

The vital teachings alone will lead into fanaticism, magnifying experiences above the Word.

When the vital aspect is understood, we know what belongs to us in Christ.

We know a Son's rights. We learn to take our place. We enjoy our privileges, and the vital side then becomes a Reality.

All that is legally, ours may become vitally ours by the ministry of the Spirit through the Word in us.

A little study of the legal side may help us.

2 Cor. 5:21, "Him who knew no sin he made to be sin on our behalf; that we might become the righteousness of God in him."

That is what God wrought in Christ.

He laid our sins upon Christ.

He was stricken, smitten of God and afflicted.

"He was wounded for our transgressions; he was bruised for our iniquities; the chastisement of our peace was upon him, and with his stripes we are healed.

"All we like sheep have gone astray; we have turned every one to his own way; and Jehovah hath laid on him the iniquity of us all."

He not only laid our sins on Jesus, but He made Jesus sin.

Rom. 3:21-26 is perhaps the great master sentence illustrating this legal side of the plan of Redemption.

He tells us in the 21st verse, "But now apart from the law a righteousness of God hath been manifested, (or unveiled; or as one translator puts it, 'brought to light') being witnessed by the law and the prophets; even the righteousness of God through faith in Jesus Christ unto all them that believe; for there is no distinction; for all have sinned, and fall short of the glory of God."

Here is a little touch of the vital in the 24th verse: "Being justified freely by his grace through the redemption that is in Christ Jesus."

In the 25th verse we swing back again to the legal: "Whom God set forth to be a propitiation," or a mercy seat where the blood was sprinkled by the High Priest, "on the ground of faith, in His blood, to show his righteousness because of the passing over of the sins done aforetime, in the forbearance of God; for the showing, I say, of his righteousness at this present season."

Here we catch a glimpse of the vital: "That he might himself be righteous, and the righteousness of him that hath faith in Jesus."

You see, the Spirit has based our present Righteousness upon the work that had been accomplished in His great Substitutionary Work.

Titus 2:14 is another scripture showing the legal side. "Who gave himself for us, that he might redeem us from all iniquity, and purify unto himself a people for his own possession, zealous of good works."

Some Vital Facts

One of the most priceless vital scriptures is 2 Cor. 5:17, 18: "Wherefore if any man is in Christ, he is a new creature: the old things are passed away; behold, they are become new. But all these things are of God, who reconciled us to himself through Christ, and gave unto us the ministry of reconciliation."

It is very important that we recognize this fact, that all that has been wrought for us by Christ in His Substitutionary Sacrifice, belongs to the individual believer.

Eph. 1:17-23 is a part of the great charter of our Redemption, and this is both legal and vital.

He reveals what He did for us.

He reveals His process of building the very Nature and Life of the Father into our spirits.

He said, I want you to know what is the exceeding greatness of His ability on our behalf who believe.

It is "according to that working of the strength of his might which he wrought in Christ, when he raised him from the dead, and made him to sit at his right hand in the heavenly places, far above all rule, and authority, and power, and dominion, and every name that is named, not only in this age, but also in that which is to come: and he put all things in subjection under his feet, and he gave him to be the head over all things for the benefit of the church, which is his body, the fulness of him that filleth all in all."

Here we have the legal background of His great Substitutionary work, of His absolutely conquering the forces of darkness before He arose from the dead.

Just as in Col. 2:15 it says, "That he put off from himself the principalities and the powers, and he made a show of them openly, triumphing over them in it."

We have failed to recognize this blessed fact, that in the Substitutionary work of Christ, it was as though we ourselves were with Him.

Just as the Spirit says in Gal. 2:20: "I was crucified with Christ," not as the old version reads, "I am crucified." No, it is past tense. It is the legal side.

He not only was crucified, but in Rom. 6:8 it says, "But if we died with Christ, we believe that we shall also live with him."

Not only were we crucified with Him but we died with Him.

In Col. 2:12 we were buried with Him.

In I Tim. 3:15 we were justified with Him.

In Col. 2:13 we were made alive with Him.

"You, I say, did He make alive together with Him."

Then in Eph. 2:6 He raised us up with Him and made us to sit with Him in the heavenlies in Christ Jesus.

In these Scriptures we get a living picture of the entire Substitutionary work of Christ, in which we have a perfect Identification. It was done for us.

It is the legal background of our Redemption.

You can say, Yes, I was crucified with Him. I was identified with Him in His shame and His deep agonies on the cross.

More than that, God not only put my sin upon Him and made

Him sin with my sin, but He put me upon Him.

He was taking my place. He was acting in my stead.

It was my sin that stripped Him naked.

It was my sin that caused the crown of thorns to be put upon His brow.

It was my sin that drove the nails into His hands and feet.

It was Love that was taking my place and suffering in my stead that I might be ransomed out of the authority of darkness and the power of sin and spiritual death.

I can say I died with Him; that when He died on the cross He partook of my spiritual death, and I was identified with Him in that spiritual death.

It was as though I had been there in person and we had left His body together.

When He died on the cross, He and I went to the place where I should have gone alone, but He went with me as my Substitute.

He went with me to suffer in my stead.

He was bearing my sin with me, that old spiritually dead self. He suffered there until the claims of Justice against me had been satisfied and there was no longer any charge against me.

My spiritual death and union with Satan were wiped out.

And then He was justified in Spirit.

His Justification was for me, for you see, He went there for me.

He didn't go there on His own account. He went on my account, and as soon as He was Justified, He was Recreated – made alive in spirit, and that wonderful scripture in Acts 13:33, "Thou art my Son, this day have I begotten thee," was made real.

Right there in those awful surroundings He was Born Again.

He had become the very Righteousness of God right there.

And now I can understand Eph. 2:10: "We are his workmanship, created in Christ Jesus."

That is the legal side of the New Birth.

In the mind of Justice, we were Recreated down there at the time Christ was, because He is the Head of the Body, the Firstborn from among the dead.

He was the first person ever Born Again. In His birth, the whole Body of Christ had the legal work accomplished for them.

Then He conquered the adversary, but in the mind of Justice I was with Him.

When He stripped Satan of his authority and dominion, it was your victory and mine.

We were there in the mind of Justice.

We put our heel upon the neck of the enemy; we stripped him of his authority; we left him defeated and broken, and then we were raised together with Christ.

Satan is conquered.

The New Birth has been accomplished.

The New Creation, in the mind of Justice, has become effective, and now we are not only raised together with Christ, but we are seated with Him.

In the mind of Justice, every member of the Body of Christ is seated at the right hand of the Majesty on high.

In the mind of Justice we are utterly one with Him. We are complete in Him.

All that He did, He did for us.

He is the Head of the Body, and as the Head of the Body, He cannot be exalted so high but what the Body is there with Him sharing in His glory, sharing in all of His victories.

Eph. 1:4-6 gives us a preview of our Redemption: "Even he chose us in him before the foundation of the world, that we should be holy and without blemish before him: in love having foreordained us unto adoption as sons through Jesus Christ unto himself. He did this according to his own good will, to the praise of the glory of his grace, which he freely bestowed on us in the beloved."

The next verse swings into the vital: "In whom we have our redemption through his blood, the remission of our trespasses, according to the riches of his grace, which he made to abound toward us in all wisdom and prudence, revealing in us the mystery of his will."

Now we can see the background of a vital union with Christ.

We can understand what it means to have him say, "For it is God who is at work within you, willing and working his own good pleasure."

We can understand Col. 1:28,29 "That we may present every man perfect in Christ: whereunto I labor also, striving according to his working, which worketh in me mightily."

Paul's dream in Christ was to present every believer perfect, "without spot or wrinkle or any such thing."

What a dream it must have been.

Now we can understand Eph. 3:16-20: "That he would grant you, according to the riches of his glory, that ye may be strengthened with power through his Spirit in the inward man."

This inner man has become a New Creation. He has received the

Life and Nature of the Father, and now the Spirit through the Word is building into this "hidden man of the heart," the ability to live as Jesus did in His earth walk.

You remember we are to walk in Love; we are to follow, after Love.

We remember that Love never faileth, and it thinketh no evil; always good thoughts, beautiful thoughts about everyone.

It never holds any enmity.

We treat the one who has lied about us, just as Jesus treated Peter after the Resurrection.

Can't you imagine Jesus hunting up the man who drove the nails into His hands and telling him "I died for you."

Finding the man that made the crown of thorns and pressed it upon His brow, telling him "I am going to give you a crown of righteousness, a crown of glory and a crown of life."

Paul said, "That Christ may dwell in your hearts on the ground of faith."

You see, Christ and the Word are one.

When the Word dwells in a believer's heart, gains control of his whole being, that is Christ gaining control. The Lordship of Jesus over a life is in Reality the Lordship of the Word. The Word gains the ascendency in such an absolute way that it dominates his thinking.

The Lordship of Jesus and the Lordship of the Word are really the Lordship of this new kind of Love – Agapa.

What beautiful lives that makes.

When this "inner man," this "hidden man of the heart" becomes governed by the Love Nature of the Father, he unconsciously takes Jesus' place.

You see, we become rooted and grounded in Agapa.

We do not hold it as a doctrine.

It is not a mental concept. It is actual.

The Father has so filled us with His Nature that we do Love acts unconsciously.

We have received the ability to understand the Nature of the Love of Christ which passeth sense knowledge apprehension, and now at last the dream of the Father for us is being fulfilled. We are filled with all the fulness of God.

The Love Nature has swallowed us up, just as 2 Cor. 5:4: "But that we should be clothed upon, that what is mortal may be swallowed up of life." Way says, "Drowned in the sea of life."

The Life is Zoe – the Nature of the Father, and the Nature of the Father is Love. We are swallowed up, immersed, overwhelmed in Love.

Now we can understand Eph. 3:20: "Now unto him that is able to do exceeding abundantly above all that we ask or think, according to the power that worketh in us."

It is the ability of the Father unveiled.

Not only is it revealed, but it is clasping the hand of Omnipotent Love; my whole inner being swinging me out of the orbit of sense knowledge into the orbit of Revelation Knowledge or Revelation Reality.

Now I know what Jesus meant when He said, "When he, the Spirit of Truth is come (or the Spirit of Reality), he shall guide you into all reality: for he shall not speak from himself; but what things soever he shall hear, these shall he speak: and he shall declare unto you the things that are to come" – the New Creation things, the unveiling of the very Nature of the Father which He declares in Christ. (John 16:13,14).

First, "He shall glorify me: for he shall take of mine, and shall declare it unto you."

This is Resurrection Life in us. This is the Holy Spirit working in us through the Word; all that was purchased for us; all that is legally ours for our daily walk.

You see, the Father had a dream for us.

In that little preview of the New Creation that I gave you, He gave us a suggestion of His intense Love for us, and how He was going to build us over into Himself.

He was going to take His Righteousness and His Holiness and His Truth or Reality and build them into us until we fit into His dream, and He could say, as He did to the wondering disciples, "This is my Beloved Son, in whom I am well pleased."

Then He would say, "These are my beloved sons, in whom my heart has found perfect rest and satisfaction."

Chapter IX

SHARING WITH HIM

N Way's Translation we get one of the richest views of Christ's ministry for us that we have in any of our translations.

Gal. 2:20, "Yes, I have shared Messiah's crucifixion. I am living indeed, but it is not I that live; it is Messiah whose life is in me."

The heart can hardly take in the reality that is unveiled to us.

"Yes, I have shared in His crucifixion."

This is the legal side of our Identification with Christ.

You see, He shared with us in His Incarnation. He became one with us.

He gave us His kingly glory and became one with suffering, lost humanity.

He was one with us in His Substitution.

He shares with us; He shares our sins, our infirmities, our diseases. He took them upon Himself.

The sharing was so real that "He who knew no sin, became sin" in order to become Identified with us, to come to our level.

He not only had sin reckoned to Him, sin laid upon Him as the High Priest laid the sin of Israel upon the goat, but He actually became sin.

We can hardly grasp the fact that Deity could become sin, but He did. He died spiritually.

"The Righteous for the unrighteous, that He might bring us to God."

In the New Creation we shared with Him.

He is the Head; we are the body.

He has imparted Himself to us, and when He imparted Himself to us, He gave to us a new self in the place of our old self.

That old, fallen, sin-ruled self was displaced and the new Jesus self, the New Creation self, the Godlike self, the self that is made in the image of Christ, became our new self.

You see how utterly He shared with us; how much He became one with us.

But in Col. 3:1 he says, "If, then, you have shared in Messiah's resurrection, aspire ever to the things on high, where Messiah is, throned at the right hand of God.

"Let your thoughts dwell on things above, not grovel on the earth. You have died to things of earth, and your real life now has been hidden, by its union with Messiah, in the being of God." (Way's Trans.)

Here we catch a glimpse of our utter oneness with Him, of the completeness of this union.

What is more real than this: "I am the vine, ye are the branches." (John 15:5).

Here He shows us we are the fruit-bearing part of Him.

We are the Love-revealing part of Him.

We are the part of Him that blesses and touches humanity.

We are the part of Him that brings Eternal Life to lost man.

We are sharing in His Resurrection.

The heart is thrilled.

If we share in His Resurrection, we share in His victory over Satan: we share in His victory over sin.

We have been raised together with Him.

We are sharing His victory over the adversary.

Then Satan knows that we conquered him in Christ, that we were with the Master when He put him to naught and triumphed over him, and put off from Himself the principalities and the powers, when Jesus made a show of Satan before his own hosts in the dark regions; that we shared with Him and were a part in that great victory.

And did you notice, we are sharing in the things on High where Messiah is enthroned at the right hand of God?

We are seated with Him.

You see, in Eph. 2:6-8 we were raised together with Him; and then not only were we raised with Him, but we were seated with Him.

Let me read from Ephesians (Way's Trans.): "Thrilled us with the same new life wherewith He quickened our Messiah. – By free grace alone have ye obtained salvation – and with Him He raised us from the dead, and with Him throned us in the high heavens."

His expression "throned us" means we are seated as one with Him on the throne now.

He is the Head of the Body; we are members of the Body. Where the Head is, the Body is.

The authority that belongs to the Head belongs to the Body.

Now you can understand Matt. 28:18: "All authority hath been given unto me in heaven and on earth." All authority; all dominion.

You understand now why He could "put off from Himself the principalities and the powers."

You can understand how He could "make a show of them."

He was the Master, with the Omnipotence and Ability of the Father.

We share in that.

He has given us the legal use of His Name. In that Name is invested all the authority the Father gave Him after His Resurrection. That Name is ours, and we have a legal right to use it.

Oh, I wish that our hearts could take it in. The days of our defeat and failure would then be over.

Rom. 6:2 (Way's Translation), throws much light upon our union with Christ. "We have passed out of sin as truly as the dead man has passed out of life: can we, when thus dead to it, still go on living in it? Or, if you fail to grasp this inference, look at it thus: do you not comprehend that all of us, who passed by baptism into union with Messiah Jesus, were by baptism made sharers in His death? Well then, if that baptism made us share His death, it must have made us share His burial too.

"It must follow that, as Messiah was raised from among the dead by means of the descent of His Father's glory, so we too, who rose with Him, are to be employed wholly in the activities of the New Life.

"For if, by having died like Him, we have entered into living union with Him, most certainly we shall not be less so in consequence of having risen with Him.

"This we recognize, that our former self was nailed to His cross with Him, so that that body which was the instrument of sin might be made impotent for evil, so that we could not any longer be slaves of sin."

Notice now from this vivid translation that we shared with Christ in His death.

We shared with Him in His Resurrection, and we are sharing now with him at the right hand of the Father.

From another angle, He is sharing with us in our ministry as branches of the Vine.

We are His testimony.

We are now His confession.

We are boldly telling the world what we are in Christ.

We have taken our place in Christ.

We are acting as a part of Himself.

We share in everything that He did. He is sharing in everything that we are.

This brings a nearness to the Reality of that great oneness between the Head and the Body.

You see, we suffered with Him; we shared in it.

We shared in His Justification.

We shared with Him when He was made alive down in that dark region, and we heard the Father whisper, "Thou art my Son; this day have I begotten thee" (Acts 13:33), speaking of His Resurrection.

We shared in that Resurrection. We shared in the power and authority of it.

When He put all the enemies beneath His feet, they were beneath our feet.

When He triumphed over them, that was our triumph.

And now we are carrying out His precious will in the earth.

He is sharing His Ability, Wisdom and Love with us.

You caught that in Rom. 6:6: We shared in His Resurrection; and in Eph. 2:5, 6, we share in His Life and we share in His throne.

In Rom. 6:8 you get it clearly: We shared in His new Life, the new Resurrection Life; the same wonderful Life that Jesus had.

Col. 2:13 (Way's Trans.) "In the rite of baptism we were laid with Him in His grave; in that rite too did we share His resurrection, through our faith in the soul-awakening power of God, who began by raising Jesus from the dead.

"And you too – for dead you lay in the charnel-house of your transgressions and the impurity of your sensual nature – you God thrilled with that same new Life of Jesus."

Can't you see the utter oneness, our absolute union in Christ?

Can't you see that today you are partaking of His Divine Nature, that as you yield to the inward Life of God in your spirit, you will slowly but surely gain the ascendency over your reasoning faculties until your mind becomes renewed through the reading of the Word, which is really the unveiling Mind of Christ.

You will have the Mind of Christ.

Don't forget for a moment that in the mind of the Father you are sharing in the Throne of Grace. You own a share in it.

Just as Way translates Eph. 2:6, "We share His throne."

Why, our Head is there. Our Lord is there. Marvelous, isn't it?

I sometimes wonder how Paul and John and the rest of them that are gathered about the Throne, feel about us down here.

I imagine Paul is just yearning over us that we might understand the riches of the unveilings that he gave to us of the Living Christ in His Resurrection.

Can't you see how we reign with Him?

In His Substitution we share with Him from the cross to the Throne.

We were crucified with Him; we died with Him; we suffered with Him; we were justified with Him; we were made alive with Him; raised with Him; and are now seated with Him.

Now you want Weymouth's translation of Rom. 5:17: "For if, through the transgression of the one individual, Death made use of the one individual to seize the sovereignty, all the more shall those who receive God's overflowing grace and gift of righteousness reign as kings in Life through the one individual, Jesus Christ."

This is the climax of our earth walk.

That overflowing Grace is the overflowing of the Love Nature of the Father that is shed abroad in our hearts by the Holy Spirit.

The Gift of Righteousness gives us our legal standing before the Father.

The overflowing Grace was the incoming of the Nature and Life, the substance and being of our Father into our spirits. The Nature of the Father coming in has made us Righteous, made us like the Father, like Jesus; made us utterly one with Him.

Now we reign as kings in the realm of this New Life through Jesus Christ our Lord.

You see, we were in slavery and servants of the adversary. We are now the joyful Love Slaves of Jesus.

We are heirs of God and joint-heirs with Christ, and we are coming into that new knowledge of what we are in Christ.

Sin-consciousness has robbed us in the past of our faith; robbed us of our sense of worthiness; robbed us of our joy of Sonship.

We know now that sin-consciousness was just a camouflage of the adversary.

We were standing complete in Christ, but we did not know it.

We were the Righteousness of God in Christ and we did not know it.

As long as Satan could keep us in ignorance, he kept us in darkness and weakness.

But the veil has been torn away. The light has shone in.

The light that we had before was darkness, but now this is the Light of Life. "He that followeth me shall not walk in the darkness."

We walked in the darkness, but now He is the Light of our Life. He is our Life. He is our Light.

We have become like those whose eyes had been blinded but now have received light, and we see things as they really are.

Before, we were groping and hoping. Now we have passed out of the realm of hope into the realm of assurance.

It is the realm of Reality.

We know who we are, what we are. We know what Grace has been bestowed upon us.

We are walking in the light of this wonderful Life Christ brought into the world.

Chapter X

THE LAW OF LIFE

THE Law of the New Covenant is a perfect contrast to the Law of the Old Covenant.

The first Covenant Law is called the "law of sin and death." The Law of the New Covenant is called the "law of the spirit of life."

One law put men in bondage; the other Law made them free from the law of sin and death.

That was a fearful title that was given to the first law – "of sin and of death."

Both sin and death are of the adversary, and so the Old Covenant Law was given to men who were governed by the adversary, who had a Satanic nature and lived in Satan's realm.

It was never given for New Creation folks.

No man that is Born Again has any part or lot in the Ten Commandments.

They were all fulfilled in Christ and set aside.

You see, He fulfilled the Abrahamic Covenant first, and after that was fulfilled, everything connected with that Covenant was set aside and finished and rolled up together in that first document.

Then Jesus inaugurated a New Covenant.

The First Covenant was sealed with the blood of bulls and goats. The Second Covenant was sealed with the blood of Jesus.

The New Creation that is under the New Covenant had a New Law given to them. Jesus gave it.

John 13:34,35, "A new commandment I give unto you, that ye love one another; even as I have loved you, that ye also love one another. By this shall all men know that ye are my disciples, if ye have love one to another."

The Pauline Epistles are a Revelation and an exposition of this New Law.

Just as Leviticus, Numbers and Deuteronomy are an exposition of the Law of the First Covenant, so these Epistles of Paul are given us to explain the New Covenant Law.

The Love Law

The 13th chapter of I Corinthians is a Revelation of what this new Love Law is, what it does, and what it does not do.

68

In Paul's other Epistles we see this New Law being demonstrated in the daily life of the New Creation.

It is very important that we understand this fact: That the New Covenant Law is not designed for men outside of Christ.

The natural man cannot obey the New Commandment that Jesus gave.

There is only one commandment to rule the New Creation, and that is, to love one another even as Jesus loved us.

That New Commandment made any other commandment absolutely unnecessary, for the man who walks in Love will never do wrong.

As Love was the fulfillment of the Old Covenant, it is also the fulfillment of the New.

Someone asks, "Why is the Mosaic Law called the 'law of sin and of death?' " Because it was to govern spiritually dead men.

The Law of the Spirit of Life is to govern Recreated men. It is the Spirit of Love.

It is the law of the very heart of Christ.

The Law that governed the dead in spirit is the Law of Moses.

It is impossible for anyone to live under the Mosaic Law today because it has been fulfilled and laid aside with the Abrahamic Covenant.

You see, "the law of the Spirit of Life" in Christ Jesus made the New Creation Jew free from "the law of sin and of death."

Gal. 3:21 "Is the law then given which could make alive, verily righteousness would have been of the law."

This is a striking sentence. If there had been a law given that could give men Eternal Life, then Righteousness would have been of the law.

"But the Scripture shut up all things under sin, that the promise by faith in Jesus Christ might be given to them that believe."

Now notice this next Scripture, "But before faith came, we (the Jews) were kept in ward under the law, shut up unto the faith which should afterwards be revealed. So that the law is become our (Jews) tutor until Christ, that we might be justified by faith."

The old version reading, "A tutor to bring us to Christ" is not correct.

The Law never brought anyone to Christ.

The Law was a "law of sin and of death."

The Holy Spirit is the only one that can bring a man to Christ.

Notice the 25th verse: "But now that faith is come, we are no longer (as Jews) under a tutor, for ye are all sons of God through faith in Christ Jesus."

I want you to notice carefully the next sentence: "For as many of you as were baptized into Christ did put on Christ. There can be neither Jew nor Greek, there can be neither bond nor free, there can be no male and female; for ye are one man in Christ Jesus."

Now you can understand I Cor. 9:19, 20 where Paul said, speaking of his ministry as a soul-winner, "For though I was free from all men, I brought myself under bondage to all, that I might gain the more.

"To the Jews I became as a Jew (when he became a New Creation he had stopped being a Jew); to them that are under the law, as under the law, not being myself under the law, that I might gain them that are under the law."

(This was written before the Temple and the whole Jewish heirarchy had been destroyed by Titus).

We must understand clearly that the moment a Gentile becomes a New Creation he stops being a Gentile.

In 1 Cor. 10:32 we have the three ethnical divisions of the human race: "Give no occasion of stumbling, either to Jews, or to Gentiles, or to the church of God."

There are no Jews or Gentiles in the Church of God. We are all one man in Christ.

The Gentile stopped being a Gentile and the Jew stopped being a Jew the moment they became New Creations.

Here is something very important.

The people who are trying to live under the Mosaic Covenant must learn this fact, that according to the Scripture I gave you from Gal. 3:21, the Law cannot give Eternal Life to man.

The Law cannot give Righteousness to man.

If the Law could have done that then Christ need not have died, because all man needed to do was to keep the Mosaic Law, the Ten Commandments, and he would be Alive and Righteous.

But because he was not Alive nor Righteous, he had to be covered with the blood of bulls and goats every year.

That blood represented life, a type of the Life of God that was to be given to the New Creation.

The Mosaic Covenant was given to a spiritually dead people.

It was a law that was to govern natural man.

Did you ever notice that the Father does not command the New Creation in Christ to love Him? Why?

He has God's Nature of Love in him and He can't help but Love Him.

He is born of Love.

Not one of the laws of the Ten Commandments fit a child of God.

There is but one law for the New Creation – "That we love one another even as Jesus loved us."

Moses' law was given by God to Israel through an angel, because God could not speak to man in any other way.

There is a suggestion in Exodus 33 that God spoke to Moses face to face, but that is the only time in all human history that God spoke to man.

So we can see there is a vast difference between the Law of Life in Christ and the Law of Death in the First Covenant.

Rom. 8:2, 3-11 has another suggestion for us, "For the law of the Spirit of life in Christ Jesus made me (as a Jew) free from the law of sin and of death."

That Scripture cannot apply to a Gentile because no Gentile was ever under the "Law of Sin and Death."

Then it shows you in the third verse the importance of the Law: "For what the law could not do, in that it was weak through the flesh, (or through the senses of spiritually dead men) God sending his own Son in the likeness of men who walk in the senses, has condemned sin in the senses, that the righteous requirements of the law might be fulfilled in us (the New Creation), who walk not after the senses, but after the Recreated spirit" (Lit.)

The Greek Word *Sarx*, as translated "flesh", should be translated "senses" every time. It makes it clearer.

Notice the fifth verse: "For they that are after the senses mind the things of the senses." Why? Because the senses are the children of the physical body.

They are the offspring of natural human life – seeing, hearing, tasting, smelling and feeling.

They convey all the knowledge to the brain that we have outside of Christ.

So they that are after the senses are ruled by the senses because they are accustomed to obeying them.

They that are after the spirit are accustomed to obeying the things of the spirit.

The word "spirit" here means the spirit of the Recreated man.

So let me read it like this: "For they that are after the senses are going to do the things that the senses suggest. But they that are after the Recreated spirit, are going to do the things of the Recreated spirit that has the Nature and Life of God in it."

Now the next verse: "For the mind of the senses is under the dominion of spiritual death, but the mind of the Recreated spirit is under the dominion of Zoe, the Life of God, and that brings peace and rest and quietness." (Lit.)

That seventh verse is suggestive: "Because the mind of the senses is enmity against God. It is not subject to the law of God, neither indeed can it be," whether it be the Law of the Ten Commandments or the Law of the New Covenant.

"For they that are living in the realm of the senses cannot please God."

Now notice this ninth verse: "But ye are not governed by the senses but by the spirit (that is, your Recreated spirit), if so be that the Spirit of God (that is, the Holy Spirit), dwelleth in you. But if any man hath not the spirit of Christ, he is none of his."

That doesn't mean the Holy Spirit. A better translation is, "If any man has not a Christlike spirit (that is, a Recreated spirit), he is none of his."

Many of our Commentators have given us a wrong conception of that. They have said, If any man has not the Holy Spirit, he is not a Christian, but that is not true.

A man can be a child of God, receive Eternal Life, and yet not have received the Holy Spirit, for you remember Luke 11:13 says, "How much more will your Heavenly Father give the Holy Spirit to them that ask him."

Only Sons will ask for the Spirit.

Acts 8:15,16, "Under Phillip's preaching, many had turned to the Lord in Samaria and had been baptized. "Then the disciples came down from Jerusalem that they might receive the Holy Spirit, for as yet he had fallen on none of them, only they had been baptized in the Name of the Lord Jesus."

They had received Eternal Life.

Then the disciples laid hands on them and they received the Holy Spirit.

When Paul came to Ephesus (Acts 19:1-7), he said to them, "Did you receive the Holy Spirit when you believed?"

The implication is simple, that all believers do not have the Holy Spirit. If they did, they would be different kind of believers, for when a man receives the Holy Spirit, he has a Teacher in him that can unfold the Word and build into him a Godlike spirituality that will make him a blessing to those around him.

Come back to Rom. 8:10, "And if Christ is in you, the body is dead because of sin: but the spirit is life because of righteousness."

Notice now, that after Christ is in you, the senses have lost their dominion over you, because when you are made a New Creation, the senses cease to be your master.

Your spirit has received Eternal Life and has become the Righteousness of God.

Sin now can no longer govern your senses.

"But if the Spirit of Him that raised Christ Jesus from the dead, dwelleth in you, (this is the Holy Spirit of whom He is speaking) he that raised up Christ Jesus from the dead, shall give life (that word life is Zoe, the Nature of God) also to your mortal body through his Spirit that dwelleth in you."

He has given to that person's spirit Eternal Life and made him a New Creation.

Now the promise that Jesus made, "I came that ye might have life, and have it abundantly," is being realized.

The Holy Spirit has come into man's body and is pouring an abundance of Life into his mortal body, bringing health and strength and vigor into it.

Now notice this fact: The New Law cannot rule spiritually dead men any more than the Ten Commandments can rule the spiritually alive man.

The First Law belonged to the old creation.

The New Law belongs to the New Creation.

This New Law of Love is to rule our daily life, our business, our homes.

It is to rule the Church.

It is to rule our social life.

This New Law is as impossible for natural man as the Mosaic Law is unnatural and abnormal for the New Creation.

The Jew under the First Covenant, could not keep the Law of the New Covenant.

So we see clearly that the Ten Commandments are for natural man.

Jesus' New Commandment was for the New Creation man.

The Love Law is to rule a New Love Creation.

It would be as absurd for citizens of the United States of America to adopt the laws of Japan and try to put themselves under them, as for Gentile men today to adopt the Ten Commandments and attempt to get God to own them as He owned the Jews under that First Covenant.

Here is a fact: The First Covenant with its commandments was never given to any nation but the Israelites.

Israel alone owned it all. For a Gentile today to call himself a Christian and attempt to live under the Abrahamic Covenant and the Mosaic Law, is the most absurd effort ever known.

Only a spiritually dead man would ever attempt it.

Chapter XI

THE RENEWED MIND

HERE has never been a great deal of teaching in regard to the necessity of a renewed mind.

We have stressed the need of being converted, being Born Again, but we have left the convert hanging in the air, as it were.

Great enthusiasm and joy comes at the New Birth, but unless that is cared for and fed by the mind being renewed through feeding on the Word and practicing it, that joy will die out.

When you are Born Again your spirit is Recreated.

It receives the Nature and Life of the Father, but the mind that has held your spirit in captivity is the same old mind.

It receives a mighty impetus when the spirit receives Eternal Life, but that is all.

You understand that all the knowledge the mind had, comes from the senses and the senses can never be renewed.

They are a part of the physical body.

They can be brought into subjection; they can be controlled, but they can't be renewed.

The spirit is Recreated, but the mind, this brain of ours that receives its knowledge from the five senses, can be brought into subjection to the Word.

I have come to believe that it can be purified by meditation in the Word.

I don't mean purified like the blood of Christ has cleansed us, but I mean that it drops off much that is unnecessary and unwise.

In itself it may not be harmful but it is unnecessary. It takes up time.

The mind slowly but surely as it feeds on the Word, meditates in the Word, practices and lives the Word, comes into the fellowship of the Recreated spirit.

In Rom. 12:1,2, we have one of the most important Scriptures in regard to the physical body and its thinking processes: "I beseech you therefore, brethren, by the mercies of God, to present your bodies a living sacrifice, holy, well-pleasing to God, which is your spiritual service."

Notice it very carefully now. He is asking you to present your body which holds the five senses.

They are the most important part of that body, the seeing part, the hearing part, the feeling part, the tasting and smelling parts.

They are the five channels to the brain over which travel all the impulses that have taught the brain all that it knows.

Now He says, I want you to give this home of your five senses to the Lord.

I want you to lay that body of yours, as it were, upon the altar.

As the Jew laid a dead offering upon the altar, you are to lay your living body upon the altar in the sense that you are dedicating it, giving it over to the Lordship of the Word.

Then He says in the second verse, "And be not fashioned according to this age, but be ye transformed (or transfigured) by the renewing of your mind, that ye may prove what is the good and acceptable and perfect will of God."

Your mind has been fashioned after the things of this world.

The world's ideals probably have been yours.

Now your mind must come under the dominion of your Recreated spirit through the Word.

Your mind must recognize the three-fold Lordship through your Recreated spirit, the Lordship of the Word, the Lordship of Jesus and the Lordship of Love.

It may be difficult for your mind to assimilate this; to allow Love to become a part of yourself: to allow the Word to utterly dominate; to recognize the Love Lordship of Jesus.

I know how hard that is, but that must come or else the believer is going to live on the borderland between right and wrong, never knowing whether this is wrong, or that is wrong.

He will be asking his friends, "Is it wrong to do this? Should I do that?"

The reason is, his mind has never been renewed and he is living on the borderland in a sort of semi-spiritual darkness.

But as his mind is renewed he will come to know the will of the Father. He will walk in the light of the Word.

He will get to know that three-fold will – the good, and the acceptable, and the perfect will of the Father.

He will be claiming the highest will of the Father.

He will not be satisfied with "the acceptable and the good," but will want the perfect and the well-pleasing will of the Father.

In John 8:28 Jesus said, "I always do the things that are pleasing to my Father."

This New Creation man craves that kind of a life.

His spirit is reaching out, sometimes really agonizing in him to become well-pleasing to the Father.

In Col. 3:5-10 He is unveiling the inner workings of the senses and their control of the mind. Read it carefully.

He says, "For which things' sake cometh the wrath of God upon the sons of disobedience."

He shows the uncleanness of the natural mind as it is dominated by the senses.

In the 9th verse He is speaking to you. He said, I don't want you to lie to one another any more, since you have put off the old man with his doings.

You see, you are a New Creation and you put on the New Man, that is being renewed in knowledge after the image of Him that created Him.

This is a message to the new convert primarily.

Old believers have already done this thing.

He wants that New Man to be brought into perfect harmony with his thinking faculties, and that can't be until his mind is renewed, until it comes to recognize its position in Christ.

You notice it said, "Put on the new man that is being renewed in knowledge after the image of Him."

That will be Revelation Knowledge.

You will know your responsibilities and your ability to meet them.

You see, the small faith man is almost invariably a man whose mind has not yet been renewed.

If you find a believer that doesn't walk in love, it is because his mind has not yet been renewed.

His mind can't be renewed by simply studying the Bible.

He will have to live it. It has to become a part of His mind.

Many of our Bible teachers have never seen this and their senses govern their mind.

That means their senses govern their teaching; that their Recreated spirit has a very small place in their lives.

2 Cor. 4:16, "Wherefore we faint not; but though our outward man is decaying, yet our inward man is renewed day by day."

The inward man is your spirit that is feeding on the Word, that is being renewed continually.

Your mind should feed on the Word too.

There should be meditation in the Word.

You remember in Joshua 1:8 Jehovah told him that he was to meditate in the word day and night, and that he might observe to do according to all that there is written therein; for then thou shalt make thy way prosperous, and then thou shalt have good success."

The same rule that God laid down for Joshua should govern the New Creation, this new man who has the mind of Christ.

Another Scripture that might help us a bit is Eph. 2:10, "For we are his workmanship, created in Christ Jesus for good works, which God afore prepared that we should walk in them."

He has prepared you to walk in His will.

His ability has been given to you.

His strength is at your disposal.

The good deeds that He would have you perform are within the range of your ability, that is, the ability that He has given to you.

He expects you to pray for sick folks.

You will teach the Word; witness to the unsaved; walk in Love, and you will walk in the light of the Word and be a blessing to those around you, because your mind now is in perfect harmony with the Recreated spirit.

The New Commandment "that you love one another" has become the very heart life of your conduct.

Chapter XII

GOD REPRODUCING HIMSELF IN US

VERY real father desires to reproduce himself in his son. The Father's dream is to reproduce Himself in us.

You understand that the New Creation has received the nature and life of the Father.

We invite the Holy Spirit, who has imparted to us this Nature from the Father, to come into our body and make His home in us, then as we begin to feed on the Word, practice the Word, live the Word, He builds that Word into us.

The very genius of Christianity is the ability of God to build Himself into us through the Word, so that in our daily walk we live like the Master.

Eph. 5:1,2 "Be ye therefore imitators of God, as beloved children; and walk in love, even as Christ also loved you, and gave himself up for us."

As children of Love, we are to walk in Love as Christ walked in Love toward the world.

The Father so loved the world that He gave His Son.

Jesus so loved the world that He gave Himself.

Now I so love the world that I give myself.

I don't allow my heart to grow bitter toward it, no matter what the criticism or the persecution may be.

Whenever I am inclined to say, Well, I am wasting my time on them, I remember Paul and Silas at Philippi. They had been arrested.

They had been whipped until their backs were a mass of bleeding flesh, then put into a dungeon with their hands and feet in stocks.

In the midst of that agony, that physical distress, they prayed and sang praises.

They so stirred Heaven that the Father had to open the jail; and when the earthquake had so frightened the jailor that he cried out in agony of fear, Paul preached to him with that bleeding back, and the jailor found Jesus.

Then he washed the backs of both Paul and Silas, and a Church was formed in the home of the jailor.

If Paul had any other spirit he could never have done it, but he was like his Master.

He gave himself up to the dominion, the Lordship of Love.

The Father wants to reproduce Himself in us.

Gal. 4:19: "My little children, of whom I am again in travail until Christ be formed in you."

The process of building Christ into one may be very slow, but it makes Jesus men and women out of us.

We are created in Christ Jesus. We are His Creation; and until Christ is formed in us, the world cannot see anything but religion in us.

Phil. 2:13: "For it is God who worketh in you both to will and to work, for his good pleasure."

The Father is actually building His Love Life, His Righteousness, His strength, and His Wisdom into our spirits.

Years ago when I was the head of the school back in the East, after an evangelistic campaign I would invariably ask some of the teachers, "Have I grown any since you last saw me? Can you see any marks of growth in my spiritual life?"

I was so fearful that a month or two would go by that I hadn't grown in Christ and in Knowledge of the Word.

2 Pet. 3:18: "But grow in the grace and knowledge of our Lord and Savior Jesus Christ."

Grace means Love at work. The Greek word means "Love Gifts."

The Spirit longs for us to grow in this Love Life; to have the Love Nature of Jesus demonstrated in our daily walk.

I am convinced beyond the shadow of a doubt, that only as we yield ourselves to the Lordship of Love, can He ever build Himself into us.

It is not knowledge of the Scriptures. "I may have a vast knowledge of the Word. That isn't it.

It is the Word that is built into me and becomes a part of me that counts.

As you study the Pauline Revelation you become convinced that the ultimate of every one of those Epistles is the building of the Jesus Life in the individual.

His plan for building Himself into us is striking.

We must take Jesus' place. We must learn to act in His stead.

There must be the conscious training of our spirits to be His actual representatives.

Col. 1:9-12 gives us an intimation of the passion of the Father to make Himself known to us in such a real way that we can enter into all the riches of the fulness of His Life that belongs to us.

Here is a prayer of the Spirit through the lips of Paul:

"For this cause we also, since the day we heard it, do not cease to pray and make request for you, that ye may be filled with the knowledge of his will in all spiritual wisdom and understanding."

The word knowledge in the Greek is "epignosis." It means full knowledge, complete knowledge, exact knowledge.

We should have that kind of Knowledge, for it is in this Revelation.

We have the Holy Spirit who inspired it as our teacher.

He has never left His position as an instructor. He is here in my heart and yours, and He longs to fill us with the exact knowledge of the Father's will in all Spiritual Wisdom and Understanding.

It will be Wisdom to use the knowledge of this Revelation in our daily walk.

It will be Wisdom to know how to use the statements of fact as well as the promises in the Gospels.

It will be Wisdom to know how to make this message known in an attractive way.

We are to have "knowledge of His will in all spiritual wisdom," a deeper insight into the very heart of the Father.

I Cor. 2:9,10 may throw some light on this. "Things which eye saw not, the ear heard not, and which entered not into the heart of man, whatsoever things God prepared for them that love him."

These are revealed to us today in this Revelation through the Spirit, for the Holy Spirit is able to search all things, yea, the deep things of God, and our recreated spirit is enabled to follow the Holy Spirit in this searching of the Riches of His Grace.

Most of these riches are in the Pauline Revelation.

In Eph. 3:8 we catch a glimpse of where Paul said, "Unto me, who am less than the least of all saints, was this grace given, to preach unto the Gentiles the unsearchable riches of Christ."

These unsearchable riches belong to us, but, like pearls, we have to search for them.

1 Cor. 2:11,12 "For who among men knoweth the things of a man, save the spirit of the man, which is in him? even so the things of God none knoweth, save the Spirit of God."

Now note carefully the next verse: "But we received, not the spirit of the world, but the Spirit which is from God; that we might know the things that were freely given to us of God. Which things also we speak, not in words which man's wisdom teacheth, but which the Spirit teacheth."

We are learning to grasp this exact truth by the aid of the Spirit.

We find that in Col. 1:9,10 this knowledge of His will in all spiritual wisdom and understanding is to enable us to walk worthy of the Lord unto all pleasing.

Our walk is before the world.

We might say that it is a two-fold walk. One phase of it is before the Father, and the other is before the world.

I am to walk worthy of the Lord before men so they will recognize this New Life in me.

I am so Jesusized (if we could coin the word), that they will become Jesus-conscious in my presence.

I knew a woman that found Christ through my ministry over the air. Her husband was a godless man and she had been a fit companion in his worldliness, but now she had found Christ.

It went on for several weeks until finally one morning before he went to work, he said, "Do you know, woman, that I have been living and sleeping and eating with Jesus Christ for the last two weeks."

She was a keen-minded woman, and she said, "How do you enjoy it?"

Tears filled his eyes. He said, "I wish I was like that. I wish I had that something that has come into your life."

You see, Jesus had so lived in her that the man could feel the presence of the Master in her.

Two young men were working in a shop. One of them was studying the Word in our classes. The fellow working on a lathe next to him said to him one morning, "Harry, I would like to ask you something that is personal. What have you in your life that makes you so different from all the other men here in the room?"

The boy answered, "Jesus." "Oh," he said, "that is religion; I don't believe in that. And the young boy said, "It is not religion, it is the Living Christ."

Christ magnified in my body, said Paul; Christ made large in my daily walk.

In Phil. 1:20, 21 he said, "For to me to live is Christ."

Once those words burned in my heart for months.

The Master was saying to me, "I want to be magnified in you. I want to absorb your personality. I want to take possession of your dreams and ambitions. I want the first place in your life."

I was afraid of Him. I spoke out, "Lord, I don't dare let you have control of me for if I do I will never achieve the things for which I am so ambitious."

And I shall never forget, a voice in my heart said, "I love you more than you love yourself. I am more ambitious for your success than you are. I have the ability to put you over."

I said, "Lord, don't make me preach on the streets. You will send me down into the slums. I don't want to go there Lord."

I struggled again, but He was tender with me.

His Wisdom became so apparent. Often in my extremities He had helped me.

When I would get into difficulties He would lift me out.

One day I said, "Master, I will go with you. Here I am; take all of my ability. Swallow up my ambition with your own, but give me Love like your Love. Help me to so live that men can see you in me, feel you, that when I speak it will be your voice. When I lay hands on the sick it will be your hands."

And then I heard a Scripture in Gal. 2:20: "I have been crucified with Christ; it is no longer I that live, but Christ liveth in me: and that life which I now live in the flesh I live in faith, the faith which is in your Master, who loved me, and gave himself up for me."

Then I said, "Now Master, I trust you and I give myself up to you.

You see, when we come quietly in our heart-life to the place where we say "Yes" to Him, then He reveals Himself in us.

It is not forced upon us. He doesn't drive us. He doesn't force us with sickness or the loss of property.

The sickness comes because we are not aware that He can shield us.

We have gone the way of our inclinations.

We have gone the way of our own desires and our plans have been worked out, reasoned out with sense knowledge.

How it must hurt His heart when we are so unwise; when we do so many foolish things.

When His Wisdom is at our call, His Ability awaits us, we are almost limitless.

All that He is is at our disposal, but sometimes we choose a road that leads to heartaches and disappointments.

You see, it is this forming of Christ within us. That is the secret that is the genius of the New Creation.

"Wherefore, if any man is in Christ, there is a New Creation."

It is perfect as far as it has gone, but He wants to build Himself more fully into that New Creation, and so He takes the things of Christ that are unveiled to us in the Word, and the Spirit builds them into us.

We admired the strength and courage of Jesus in His earth walk.

We were thrilled at the ability that Christ manifested as He met every difficult situation.

His Wisdom, gentleness and forbearance we admired, and now the Spirit wants to take all of those things that we have admired in Jesus and build them into us.

Can't you see what it means? It is the Father's ambition to make us successful and to enable us to enjoy the riches that belong to us.

I don't know whether you have noticed it or not, but in one of the prayer Scriptures in John 16:23,24, Jesus said this: "And in that day ye shall not pray to me. (This is literal).

"But verily, verily, I say unto you, if ye shall ask anything of the Father, He will give it to you in my name.

"Hitherto have ye asked nothing in my name: ask, and ye shall receive, that your joy may be made full."

Joy is something that comes into the Recreated human spirit. The natural man doesn't have it.

Hear Jesus speaking again in John 15:11: "These things have I spoken unto you, that my joy may be in you, and that your joy may be made full."

That is a miracle, that Jesus' joy may be made full in me.

That not only will I make Him joyful, but He imparts to me His joy.

That something that makes the evangel irresistible, now fills my heart. When I speak my face will glow, my voice will be filled with the melody of heaven.

You see, when He builds himself into us and we begin to labor together with Him, we have His Life, we have His Love, yea, we have Himself.

Christ then is being formed in us.

Now it is no longer I but Christ.

The men who have grown deeply spiritual, are the men in whom the Word has had full control.

John 15:7,8 may throw a little light on this: "If ye abide in me, and my words abide in you."

Every believer is in Christ, but His words are not in every believer.

What does it mean to have His words abiding in me, gaining the absolute ascendency, dominating me in every phase of my thinking and my life.

As Jeremiah said, We feed upon the Word of God. Now I am feeding. I am living in that Word. I am practicing it. I am what James (1:22, 23) calls, "a doer of the Word."

Jesus said that the doer of the Word dug deep and built his house upon the rock, and it made his house able to stand against any storm that might beat against it.

He not only said that, but He said "If ye abide in me, and my words have found their place in you, then you can ask what you will and it shall be created by the Father for you," – brought into being.

Oh, I see it now. I cooperate with him.

In that fifth verse he said, "I am the vine, ye are the branches." Now I can understand it.

As a branch, I am going to bear His fruit. I am laboring together with Him. He and I are operating together, are identified one with the other.

He is finding a place for His ability to energize and act here on the earth again.

It is like a wealthy man that finds an intelligent, young man that he can set up in business, and the young man has ability to use this wealthy man's money.

Now He and I are laboring together and the Father is glorified because I am bearing much fruit, and I prove by my life my discipleship.

I prove that I am growing in Grace, and I am growing in that "exact knowledge of God, in all spiritual Wisdom and Understanding, to the end that I may walk worthy of the Lord unto all pleasing."

I am bearing fruit now in every good work, and I am increasing in that exact knowledge, that perfect knowledge of the Father.

You have noticed in Jesus' life that there was always a sense of sureness, a sense of certainty. There was no vacillating.

He never stopped and said, "Now pray that I may have wisdom." He had it.

Into our lives comes that same quiet sureness, that certainty that we know the Father's will. We are walking in it.

And we are made fruitful with His ability that is at work in us. It is according to the might of His glory, and it has given to us steadfastness and long-suffering, with joy.

Col. 1:12: "Giving thanks unto the Father, who has given us the ability to enjoy our share of the inheritance of the saints in light."

This is a climax of the heart desire of the Father that we should so let Him live His Life in us, that we begin to enjoy our share of our inheritance in Christ.

We are drawing dividends on what He has done for us and in us.

We are coming to enjoy the riches of His Grace.

Chapter XIII

LIMITING GOD IN US

THE Spirit speaking through Paul in Phil. 2:13 says, "For it is God who is at work within you, willing and working his own good pleasure" (Literal).

How hard it has been for some of us to become God-inside-minded, to daily remind ourselves that we have Him in us, and that He is there to build Christ into us, to build the Living Word into us.

Just as a mason builds a house brick by brick, so the Holy Spirit will take one truth after another and build it into us until we become Jesus-minded, Love-controlled, Father-pleasers.

You remember in John 8:29 Jesus said, "For I do always the things that are pleasing to him."

For years that was my heart's slogan.

I sought to make Him happy.

You see, He has done a perfect work for us in the great Substitution. There is not a thing left undone.

If we accept that work and let God work in us, it makes us stand well pleasing before the Father.

We become beautiful to Him because His Nature was not only given to us, but now He has built into us through the Spirit the new habits that belong to the Family of God, the new language that belongs to the New Creation.

We never talk doubt or fear or sickness or want.

We have almost forgotten that language.

We have the new language of the overcomer; the language of the man who is tied up with Christ.

It is the language of the branches of the Vine.

That Vine Life has so developed in us that we become Jesus men and Jesus women.

In our assembly in Seattle, we speak of them as the Jesus men and Jesus women.

We have Jesus men and women who are going out into the world, touching it, blessing it, illuminating it with the Life of Christ in them.

Why can't this spread over the land until there arises a new race of men known as the Jesus Folks.

They will be Love in action.

They will be living in the Word and the Word will be living in them.

They will be doing the works of the Master.

As Jesus did physical healing and ministered largely in the sense realm, these Jesus folks will minister very largely in the spiritual realm.

2 Cor. 9:8-12 "And God is able to make all grace abound unto you; that ye, having always all sufficiency in everything, may abound unto every good work."

How slow we have been to realize that it was God's Ability that could make Grace abound in and through us, and that we were being so perfectly supplied by Him that we were having all sufficiency in everything.

He is our sufficiency; He is our ability; He is the strength of our lives.

We have ignored sense reasoning and cast it down and have given our Recreated spirits the right of way and the Word the first place.

Notice this tenth verse: "And he that supplieth seed to the sower and bread for food, shall supply and multiply your seed for sowing, and increase the fruits of your righteousness: ye being enriched in everything unto all liberality, which worketh through us thanksgiving to God."

There has been little majoring of the fruit of Righteousness.

I have been asked again and again, what does it mean?

(It means that same kind of fruit that we saw in Jesus' public ministry.)

You see, Righteousness means the ability to stand in the Father's presence without the sense of guilt or condemnation or inferiority.

It means the ability to stand in the presence of Satan and his works without timidity or fear, without any sense of inferiority.

Really, it means that you have become superior to Satan.

You have a superiority complex rather than an inferiority complex.

You have come to reckon on the ability of the God inside of you.

You have at last arrived at the place where you reckon on Him.

You plan your work with the idea that He is there to enable you to put it over.

We must not omit Eph. 1:19-23. I want this Scripture to become so familiar to you that it will be a constant source of comfort and strength.

He said: "I want you to know what the exceeding greatness of the ability of God is on our behalf who believe. That ability is according to the strength of his might, which he wrought in the Christ when he raised him from the dead." (Lit.)

You can't over-estimate this.

This is God working within you.

This is the one who raised Jesus from the dead.

This is the one who Recreated you.

This is the Spirit who has all the ability of the God-head that is necessary for you to enjoy; so that you are not afraid of the enemy in any field.

You know He put all things in subjection under His feet, and He gave Him to be head over all things for the benefit of the Church.

Remember, this is the One who is at work within you.

Take Eph. 3:20 "Now unto him that is able to do exceeding abundantly above all that we ask or think, according to the ability of God that is at work within us."

When this Scripture is understood, put into daily practice, you can know that you have arrived.

At last you are a worthy member of the Vine. You are actually bearing fruit to His glory.

In my notes I have written this: Becoming God-inside-minded, knowing that the Allwise One is in me now.

That the God of all ability is in me now.

That the God of all Love is in me now.

That God and I are linked up together, laboring together with Him.

We are becoming one in our thoughts and in our actions.

He and I are laboring together to carry out the great dream of Grace.

The God of all Grace lives in me, and so I say it over and over again, "God, my Father, in the person of the Holy Spirit, through the Living Word, is living in me."

Now I can do all things in Him because he has become my strength and my ability.

The Limitless One is in me.

The Love God lives in me.

At last I become God-inside-minded.

I John 4:4 is not only a Scripture, but it is a Living Reality. "Ye are of God, my little children, and have overcome them: because greater is he that is in you than he that is in the world."

The God of Abundant Life is in me.

He is no longer with me to convict me, but He is in me to guide me into all the Realities of His mighty ministry.

Now I can understand what He meant when He said, "Laboring together with Him."

I can understand what it means when He said in I Cor. 3:9: "For we are God's fellow-workers: ye are God's husbandry, God's building."

I know what it means now to be a fellow-worker.

I know what it means to be God's tilled land (margin).

My heart and my life are the soil where He sows the seeds of Love and they are growing now in me.

I am a part of God's dream and plan.

I am coming to appreciate what it means to have real, intimate fellowship with Him.

Chapter XIV

WHAT WE DARE CONFESS ABOUT OURSELVES

ERHAPS we have never majored in our own thinking, in our own inner consciousness, what we really are in Christ; what it means to have Jesus as the Lord of our lives.

We read in Paul's or John's Epistles what they say about it.

John said, "Beloved, now are we the sons of God."

Again, "He that is born of God overcomes the world."

We never associated that with ourselves.

We never seriously said, Well, John is talking about me now. Or, Paul is describing me.

You know this Pauline Revelation is like a family album. We pick it up and look at the first picture taken of us when we were but a babe.

I turn again and I see another picture.

Months have passed since that first one was put in the album, and I see that someone has written underneath it, "When by reason of time ye ought to be teachers, ye have need now that someone teach you the first principles of the rudiments of Christ; you still have to be fed on milk and not on the solid food."

And I notice further: He calls my attention to the fact that I have never taken advantage of my Righteousness.

I have lived as "a mere man", when in reality I was a partaker of the Divine Nature.

I remember how all these months I had been afraid to acknowledge that I was a Christian.

I had not taken my stand.

My confession had been very uncertain, indefinite. Why?

Because I had not studied to show myself approved unto God.

I had not lived the Word.

I had not practiced the Word, and so I dared not confess that I was what the Word said I was.

The Word says I am redeemed. "In whom I have my Redemption."

But I have no sense of Redemption. Satan rules over me.

I live a great deal like those about me.

I go to the same places they go.

I listen to their stories and talk.

I go to church, and when they preach a real heart-searching message and give an altar call, I usually go to the altar.

I cry a little and feel mighty sorry that I haven't done any better, but I go out and go back into my old life.

Ah yes, I have Eternal Life, I know that.

I remember back yonder when one night God gave me Eternal Life and for a few months I lived in heaven. I had wonderful victory and led several people to Christ.

Then something happened and darkness came down over my life and since that time I have never walked in the light. I did not know how to do it.

I wish I did know how to get back into the old joy I once had.

And then someone whispers to me and says, Haven't you read in I John 1:9, "If we confess our sins, he is faithful and righteous to forgive us our sins, and to cleanse us from all unrighteousness"?

I answer, "Yes, I know that Scripture. I have done it again and again but I get no relief."

But the same voice whispers again, "Read it once more. 'If we confess our sins'. You did that"? "Yes." "What does it say next?" "He is faithful and just (or righteous) to forgive us our sins."

Well, if you have asked His forgiveness, don't you think He is faithful and righteous enough to make His Word good in your case?

I wait a moment and I look into that Word again and read it once more: "Faithful and righteous to forgive us our trespasses", and my heart leaps for joy.

Why, He has forgiven me! That lost fellowship is restored.

I see it now. I have lived in darkness all these months, when I could have walked in the light as He is in the light. I could have had fellowship with the brethren, and fellowship with Heaven and I didn't know it.

But I know it now, and before the world I confess that I am walking in the light.

I confess that God is my Father and I am His child; that I am in His Family.

Satan's dominion over me has been broken, and I have in me now the very Nature and Life of the Son of God. He gave it to me.

I am a partaker of the Divine Nature.

I have passed out of death into Life.

I know I am a Son of God, and if I am a Son, then I am an heir and a joint-heir with Jesus Christ.

If that is true, then I have a standing with the Father just like the Master had, because He has become my sponsor. He is my Savior and my Lord.

I see it now. He has made me His Righteousness, and I can now stand in the Father's presence just as I did in those first glad days after I accepted Him.

I have a right now to ask Him to come into my body and make it His home.

I remember He said, "If a man loves me, he will keep my word, and the Father and I will love him, and we will come and make our abode with him."

I wonder if that doesn't mean that He will come and live in me?

Wouldn't it be wonderful if He would live in my body, so wherever I went He would be with me; He would be in me.

Then Isa. 41:10 becomes a reality: "Fear thou not, for I am with thee; be not dismayed, for I am thy God; I will strengthen thee: yea, I will help thee; yea, I will uphold thee with the right hand of my righteousness."

This is mine, all mine, and I dare confess it before the world.

Wonderful thing, isn't it?

Rom. 8:11 at last is real: "But if the Spirit of him that raised up Jesus from the dead dwelleth in you, he that raised up Christ Jesus from the dead shall make his home in your body."

Yes, quicken your body; heal it if it is sick; make it strong if it is weak, and pour into your spirit the consciousness of a victor, the sense of an overcomer.

Heb. 13:20 then becomes a living Reality: "Now the God of peace, who brought again from the dead the great shepherd of the sheep, with the blood of an eternal covenant, even our Lord Jesus, make you perfect in every good thing to do his will, working in you that which is well pleasing in his sight."

How vividly real this can become to the heart, and it all comes when one dares to confess what he is in Christ; and more than that: confess it in the face of everything.

Chapter XV
WHAT REPENTANCE MEANS

THE problem of repentance in the face of modern preaching is a serious one.

The meaning of the word that was used by Peter on the day of Pentecost (Acts 2:38): "Repent and be immersed every one of you in the name of Jesus Christ unto the remission of your sins; and ye shall receive the gift of the Holy Spirit."

The Greek word means a "change of principle and practice," "A mental change of attitudes." Another, "a change of mind"; "a change of one's mode of thinking," "of one's conduct." Hold these definitions clearly in your mind as we study the Word.

It will be necessary for us first to notice the actual condition of natural man.

The Real Condition of Natural Man

I Cor. 2:14: "Now the natural man receiveth not the things of the Spirit of God: for they are foolishness unto him; and he cannot know them, because they are spiritually understood."

Why is it impossible for the natural man to understand the things of God?

Eph. 2:1-3 will give us a suggestion: "And you did he make alive, when ye were dead through your trespasses and sins, wherein ye once walked according to the course of this age, according to the prince of the powers of the air, of the spirit that now worketh in the sons of disobedience; among whom we also all once lived in the lusts of our flesh, doing the desires of the flesh and of the mind, and were by nature children of wrath, even as the rest."

Now we will notice it more fully as we go on. Here we found first, that the natural man is dead in trespasses and sins. What does it mean?

Perhaps we may get a suggestion from John 5:24: "Verily, verily, I say unto you, He that heareth my word, and believeth him that sent me, hath eternal life, and cometh not into judgment, but hath passed out of death unto life."

What does he mean by death?

There are two kinds of death mentioned in the Word – physical death and spiritual death.

Spiritual death is the nature of Satan, just as Spiritual Life is the Nature of the Father.

I John 3:14,15 will throw more light upon this. "'We know that we have passed out of death into life, because we love the brethren. He that loveth not abideth in death. Whosoever hateth his brother is a murderer: and ye know that no murderer hath eternal life abiding in him."

Here we have the contrast of death and life. Life is the Nature of the Father; death is the nature of the enemy, for the natural man is spiritually dead.

He is a partaker of Satanic nature that was given to him in the Garden, and down through the ages spiritual death has dominated man.

If you wish to see a vivid contrast, turn to Rom. 5:17 in Weymouth's Translation. "For if, through the transgression of one, death seized the sovereignty through the one, much more shall they that receive the abundance of grace and the gift of righteousness reign as kings in the realm of life, through the one Jesus Christ."

Spiritual death seized the sovereignty over the human race in the Garden and man served as a slave under its dominion.

Paul unveils to us in Rom. 5:12-21 the whole drama of spiritual death. Read this: "Therefore, as through one man sin entered into the world, and death (spiritual death) through sin; and so death passed unto all men, for that all sinned."

The fourteenth verse: "Nevertheless death reigned as a king over them that had not sinned after the likeness of Adam's transgression."

What does he mean? That physical death reigned over all men? No, spiritual death.

It had reigned without interference until Moses came.

What did Moses give? Moses gave us the atonement in the blood of bulls and goats.

Atonement means to cover.

He took a garment of animal life and spread it over spiritually dead Israel. That garment of blood covered the broken law and the priesthood.

Spiritual death lost its complete sovereignty as long as Israel walked in the First Covenant, but when Jesus came, the combat was between Life and Death. Not physical life nor physical death, but the new kind of life that Jesus brought was at war with spiritual death.

In John 10:10 he says, "I am come that ye may have life, and may have it in abundance."

The Greek word translated Life is "Zoe," which means God's Nature, God's substance, God's being, just as spiritual death means Satan's substance, Satan's being.

Out of Eternal Life have sprung all the beautiful graces which adorn a Christian life.

Out of spiritual death, the garden plot of sin, have grown all the sins that have ever been committed.

Man is united to Satan spiritually.

Perhaps the most awful words that Jesus ever uttered to the Jews, are recorded in John 8:44,45: "Ye are of your father, the devil, and the lusts of your father it is your will to do. He was a murderer from the beginning, and standeth not in the truth, because there is no truth in him. When he speaketh a lie, he speaketh of his own: for he is a liar, and the father thereof.

This is a heart-searching Scripture.

Satan was a murderer and a liar. He was a murderer by nature.

The very substance and being of Satan are the very opposite of what we see in the man Jesus.

Jesus is Truth. He is Life. He is Love.

Satan is spiritual death. He is a hater, a sin-producer. He is everything that is bad.

Jesus was everything that was good.

I John 3:10 carries us a step farther in this unhappy drama: "In this the children of God are manifest, and the children of the devil."

Here we have the two families in contrast – the Family of God and the family of the devil.

Eph. 2:11,12 gives us one of the saddest pictures of the natural man. The Spirit through Paul is speaking: "Wherefore remember, that once ye, Gentiles in the flesh, who are called Uncircumcision by that which is called Circumcision," that is, the Jews called the Gentiles the Uncircumcision. Why?

Because the circumcised man was in the First Covenant and had Covenant rights and Covenant privileges, but the Gentile man, the uncircumcised, was outside.

The Jew would not eat at the same table with the Gentile, as he was considered unclean. The next verse explains it:

"That ye were at that time separate from Christ, alienated from the commonwealth of Israel, and strangers from the covenants of promise, having no hope and without God in the world."

All of God's blessings are wrapped up in Christ.

The Gentile is separated from Christ.

Second fact: He is alienated even from the commonwealth of Israel, the covenant people that have covenant claims on God, and he is a stranger from any covenant relationship with God or contract with God.

He has no hope; he is without God, and he is in the world.

Notice his condition now: He is spiritually dead, united with Satan.

Jesus calls him a child of the devil.

John the Baptist, you remember, said "Ye vipers. He meant, children of Satan.

He has no Covenant claims on God. He is without hope, hopeless; without God, Godless, and he is here in the world.

2 Cor. 4:3,4 reveals more fully his desperate condition "And even if our gospel is veiled, it is veiled in them that perish; in whom the god of this world hath blinded the minds of the unbelieving, that the light of the gospel of the glory of Christ, who is the image of God, should not dawn upon them."

This scripture hurts. Here the curtain is lifted.

This spiritually dead man is mentally blinded, spiritually blinded.

I do not know how clearly you understand it, but all the knowledge that this spiritually dead man has, comes through the five senses: Seeing, hearing, tasting, smelling and feeling.

There is no other way for natural man to get knowledge. His body has been his laboratory.

I sometimes think of it as just physical body knowledge.

That is all the natural man has.

Is it any wonder that Darwin gave us the hypothesis of Evolution.

Sense knowledge can never find God.

Sense knowledge cannot understand spiritual things, and this sense knowledge man ruled by the senses, governed by the senses, is spiritually blinded.

If, you want to know more fully about him, turn to Eph. 4:17: "And this I say therefore, and testify in the Lord, that ye no longer walk as the Gentiles also walk, in the vanity of their mind, being darkened in their understanding, alienated from the life of God, because of the ignorance that is in them, because of the hardening of their heart."

A man may be the head of a University, but he is lost, without God and without hope.

This is a series of Love's photographs of natural man.

(Read my book "Two Kinds of Knowledge").

Now let us go back and look at repentance again.

The preacher is demanding that this natural man "change his mind and purpose," or "change his principles and practice"; "change his mode of conduct"; give up his old habits; give up his rebellion against Divine authority.

The question is, Can he do it?

Will crying and weeping and praying change his nature? Understand, he is by nature a child of wrath. He can't change his own nature.

He may change his mind for a moment but it will come back again.

What he must have is a New Nature, and this must come from God.

How can he get this New Nature?

Turn with me to John 3:16: "For God so loved the world, that he gave his only Begotten Son, that whosoever believeth on him should not perish, but have Eternal Life.

"For God sent not his Son into the world to condemn the world, but that the world should be saved through him."

What is it that the natural man needs?

It is Eternal Life, the Nature of God, and he can't get this by any effort of his own.

He cannot change his nature.

He may give tip some of the habits that he has learned, but that does not save him.

Let us go back and notice it once more.

He in himself has no approach to God.

He is an eternal being, but a hopeless one.

His nature is enmity toward God. Satan has blinded his mind.

His senseless heart is darkened. Satan has ruled him through his senses.

Love has given Jesus to him. Love has done more than that.

Rom. 4:4,5 "Now to him that worketh, the reward is not reckoned as of grace, but as of debt. But to him that worketh not, but believeth on him that justifieth the ungodly, his faith is reckoned for righteousness."

What does he mean here?

He means one who does not attempt to make himself better or who tries to give up his old habits and his old life, but accepts the gift God has given to him without money and without price, receives Eternal Life. His old habits stop being and new habits take their place.

Rom. 4:25, speaking of Jesus, "Who was delivered up on the account of our trespasses, and was raised when he was justified."

What does that mean? It means that Jesus actually suffered until every claim of Justice was satisfied as far as the sinner was concerned.

And the second thing, when the claims of Justice were met, He was raised to prove that He had paid the penalty of our trespasses, and now man has Justification, Righteousness and Eternal Life awaiting him.

Being therefore Justified by Faith, or being therefore declared Righteous on the ground of pure Grace, God says to the sinner, Take Jesus as your Saviour, confess Him as Your Lord, and I will give you Eternal Life and make you a New Creation.

You see this is all of Grace.

When I tell the unsaved man that he must have godly sorrow and repentance, I don't know what I am talking about.

Paul told that Christian young man that had committed an unwholesome sin, that he needed godly sorrow that would work a repentance in his own life.

That message can be preached to the Church today.

The Church needs to repent.

The unsaved man needs to take Jesus as his Savior and confess Him as his Lord.

The unsaved man needs Eternal Life and Righteousness.

Eph. 2:10: "For we are his workmanship created in Christ Jesus."

When were we created in Christ Jesus?

After He had been made sin on our behalf and was made alive.

When the Father justified Him in spirit down there in the place of suffering and made Him alive, the Church was Justified.

There the Church was made alive in spirit with Him, or Re-created in the mind of the Father.

Now the unsaved man receives that Eternal Life and Righteousness and comes into the Family of God.

They are awaiting him. The thing has all been done. The Father's work in Christ is finished.

When Jesus sat down on the right hand of the Majesty on High, it was because He had finished the work of Redemption.

There was no more work to be done. Redemption was a settled and fixed thing.

Now I accept it and come into the benefits of the finished work of my Lord.

You see, Jesus belongs to the unsaved man.

The unsaved man has Jesus on his hands. He died for him.

He put sin away for him.

He has made the New Birth a possibility for him, but the unsaved man must accept Him.

Rom. 10:9,10 tells us, "Because if thou shalt confess with thy mouth Jesus as Lord, and shalt believe in thy heart that God raised him from the dead, thou shalt be saved; for with the heart man believeth unto righteousness; and with the mouth confession is made unto salvation."

With his lips he makes confession of his salvation.

Now notice it carefully. Jesus belongs to him but He is of no value to him until he confesses His Lordship over his life.

Eternal Life belongs to him but he never gets it.

He never has any benefit from, it until he accepts Christ as his personal Savior and confesses His Lordship.

Then he becomes a New Creation in Christ Jesus.

The old things pass away just the moment Eternal Life comes into his spirit.

Moody used to declare that repentance meant "right about face." That is true.

The moment that the sinner accepts Jesus Christ he does a right about face.

But he can't do it unless he accepts what God has wrought for him in Christ.

The unsaved man has the ability to confess Jesus Lord over his life with his lips.

He has the ability to make the decision, to take Christ as his Savior.

God's hands are tied until he does make that confession.

He doesn't ask a sinner to confess his sins.

That is a self-evident fact.

He is a sinner, but God demands that he confess the Lordship of Jesus, and when he does that, he confesses his faith in the Substitutionary work that Christ wrought on his behalf.

Now you can understand Eph. 2:4-10: "But God being rich in mercy, for his great love wherewith he loved us, even when we were dead through our trespasses, made us alive together with Christ (by grace have ye been saved), and raised us up with him, and made us sit with him in the heavenly places, in Christ Jesus: that in the ages to come he might show the exceeding riches of his grace in kindness toward us in Christ Jesus: for by grace have ye been saved through faith; and that not of yourselves, it is the gift of God: not of works, that no man should glory. For we are his workmanship, created in Christ Jesus."

We should make the message so clear and simple that the unsaved man can see Jesus as his Savior and Lord.

We should make the message so easy to grasp that he can see that all he needs to do is to act upon the Word.

Do not tell him he needs to believe.

Do not tell him he needs to repent for that will confuse him.

If he accepts Christ as his Savior and confesses Him as his Lord, that is repentance. That is all God requires.

Chapter XVI

HAVING YOUR OWN FAITH LIFE

T IS an unhappy thing to be dependent upon another's faith. In a measure we are all dependent upon others, but in this vital issue of life, no believer should be dependent upon another's ability to approach the Throne.

We cannot afford to trust others with vital issues that we ourselves should be able to face.

Faith is measured by our appreciation of our position in the Father's Family.

When we know our place as a child, know our rights, know our Righteousness, our Ability to stand in the Father's presence without the sense of guilt or inferiority, when we know that we have as good a standing before the Father as Jesus had in His earth walk, then the problem of faith is settled.

I Cor. 1:30 should be a prominent Scripture in our daily walk. "But of him are ye in Christ Jesus, who was made unto us wisdom from God, and righteousness and sanctification, and redemption."

We need a consciousness of both Righteousness and Wisdom.

We need to know He is now our Righteousness, and that 2 Cor. 5:21, "Him who knew no sin he made to be sin on our behalf; that we might become the righteousness of God in him," has become a Reality.

You see, we have absolutely become, by the New Birth, by our being partakers of the Divine Nature, the very Righteousness of God in Christ.

That is not philosophy nor theology, it is a fact.

Just as hunger and thirst are facts, our Righteousness and our standing before the Father is a definite, clear-cut Reality.

Jesus was made unto us Wisdom at the same time He was made unto us Righteousness.

We desperately need Wisdom to use our Righteousness and to use the ability that has been given to us in Christ.

Eph. 4:7 states a fact that has been ignored by the average believer. "But unto each one of us was the grace given according to the measure of the gift of Christ."

Grace means ability. Grace means everything that we need in this earth walk.

But we have lacked the Wisdom to utilize our abilities, to take advantage of our position in Christ.

Now Jesus is made unto us Wisdom.

Every believer ought to know that, just as they know they have an umbrella or a raincoat during the rainy season, and before they start out, they put on their rubbers, don their raincoats, and take their umbrella and go to the office.

When you go out in the morning to face life's hard problems, you should remember these facts:

You have His Wisdom now to meet every need of today.

You have to meet a number of people. Some of them are going to be very difficult, but you have His Wisdom and His Ability to make the contacts and go through the business successfully.

You have Wisdom superior to theirs. They have nothing but material, human wisdom. You have His Wisdom.

He has been made unto you Wisdom.

Not only that, but you are His Righteousness.

That gives you access to the Throne at any time.

You can stand in His presence just as Jesus did in His earth walk, because Jesus is your Righteousness.

There can be no event so great but what His Wisdom and His Righteousness will enable you to meet it successfully.

You see, when you become the Righteousness of God, that really makes you a Master of Circumstances.

That lets you into the Inner Circle.

That gives you the advantage of the Father's Wisdom and Ability to put you over.

Satan cannot cope with the man who knows he is the Righteousness of God in Christ, who knows that Jesus has been made unto him Wisdom.

That man is a Master man.

You see, that leads you into the Superman Realm.

Take account of stock for a moment.

You have God's very Nature in you.

The old life that kept you in bondage has stopped being.

The old self that was dominated by circumstances and by Satan has stopped being, and a New Self, a dominant Self, a Righteous Self, a God-filled Self has taken its place.

You now have a legal right to the use of Jesus' Name.

Before the Master ascended, you remember He said in Matt. 28: 18, "All authority has been given unto me in heaven and on earth."

That authority is for the Members of the Body.

Jesus doesn't need it.

He and the Father are one, so all that the Father is, Jesus is.

This authority was given to the Church.

The ability to use that authority is given to us in the Holy Spirit.

We not only have this authority, but we have the great Mighty Spirit who raised Jesus from the dead dwelling in us, and when He came into us, He brought all His Ability, the Ability that He exercised in the resurrection of the Master, the Ability that He exercised in Christ. It is all in Him.

No wonder John said by the Spirit, in John 4:4, "Greater is he that is in you than he that is in the world."

You see, we are dominant people. We have the creative Ability of God in us.

No limit to where we can go.

It is not only these abilities, but there are other abilities that are ours.

"Of His fulness, have we received."

Perhaps among the most important assets that we have is the new kind of Love.

Jesus brought it into the world.

When we are Recreated, that new kind of Love becomes our Nature.

We become partakers of the Divine Nature, for the Father is Love.

When that Love Nature comes in, it brings an element into a man that makes him a Master.

When a man loses his temper, the person that caused him to lose his temper is superior to him in some way.

He wouldn't lose his temper if that person hadn't outwitted him, out-generalled him in some way.

Love makes us impervious to these influences, makes us a Master of them.

We rise up in God, that is, we rise up in Love; we walk in Love; we live in Love, and that makes us Masters of every person that does not walk in Love.

The unpleasant things that he does or says, we know are said by an inferior.

Love never becomes irritated.

Love never loses its poise; never loses its temper.

It is Master of itself, and that makes it Master of every person outside of Love.

This Jesus nature makes you a dominant personality, a Master personality.

They can't conquer you any more than they could conquer Christ.

They may stone you; they may beat you; they may, because of numbers, take you captive, but you become their Master the moment you become their captive. It is a strange fact, but it is true.

His Love Nature makes you a Master.

I want you to learn to believe in Love.

I want you to learn to rest in it, to depend on it, to expect great things from it. You will not be disappointed.

You remember that passage, "Ye are of God my little children." That is I John 4:4, and then in John 3:5-8 Jesus said, "Except a man is born of water and the Spirit, he cannot enter into the kingdom of God. That which is born of the flesh is flesh."

Then He says another startling thing: "That which is born of the Spirit is spirit."

Well, then you do not belong to the old order of things. You belong to this New Family, this new condition.

You are a partaker of the Divine Nature.

You are in the realm of Life with God, and you reign as a king in this realm of Life.

You are a Master. What makes you a Master?

The very nature of the Father that has come into you.

This Love gift has made you superior to everything surrounding you.

The forces that surround you, emanate from the selfishness of natural man.

You now have the Love Nature of God. That makes you superior.

You must learn to trust this. Think about what you are in Christ.

Never think of your lack; think of the vast inheritance that is yours, for you know that He has given you the ability to enjoy all that belongs to you.

Let me give you Col. 1:12: "Giving thanks unto the Father, who has given us the ability to enjoy our share of the inheritance of the saints in light."

You have the Ability to enter into all the fulness of Christ.

John 1:16 means nothing unless you take advantage of it. "Of his fulness have we all received, and grace upon grace."

That was not said for angels nor for men during the millennium; that is for us now.

You have His fulness. It may be an undeveloped property in you.

You may never have taken advantage of the riches of the glory of your inheritance in Christ.

You may have stayed in the babyhood realm where you are always struggling and trying to get something and to be something.

You have passed that; you are something.

He has made you to be what you are in Christ.

You see, you were Created in Christ.

Eph. 2:10 ought to solve every problem of our spiritual conflict. "For we are his workmanship, created in Christ Jesus for good works, which God afore prepared that we should walk in them."

There is no limit to your walk and to your ability.

The only limit is the limit you set, and just as soon as you take your hands off of this New Creation and let it function and develop in Christ, you become at once an outstanding blessing to the world.

You have an unconscious fellowship with the Father and with Christ.

That fellowship is three-fold: It is with the brethren who walk in the light, and oh, what a heavenly thing that is; Walking in fellowship with those whom you love and who love you and love our Lord.

Second, it is with Christ as Lord. 1 Cor. 1:9, "He has called us unto fellowship with His Son."

Third, you have fellowship with the Word. The Word becomes to us the very voice of the Master.

It speaks to you; it strengthens you; it comforts you.

You read a passage like this in Col. 1:27: "To whom God was pleased to make known what is the riches of the glory of this mystery among the Gentiles, which is Christ in you, the hope of glory."

You have the riches of His very Ability in you.

Or take this one in Col. 2:6: "Therefore as you receive Christ Jesus the Lord, so walk in him, rooted and builded up in him, and established in your faith, even as ye were taught, abounding in thanksgiving."

You are in it; you are a part of it. It is yours.

You are not struggling for anything.

You have entered into your Rest.

He has become your Ability for every emergency.

There was a time when you struggled and prayed and groaned to be something.

But Col. 3:1, 2 is a photograph of yourself: "If then ye were raised together with Christ, seek the things that are above, where Christ is, seated on the right hand of God.

"You have set your mind on the things that are above, not on the things that are on the earth."

And then He tells us Christ is our Life.

We are absolutely one with Him.

He has become a part of us and we have become a part of Him.

We have learned what John 8:12 means: "I am the light of the world: he that followeth me shall not walk in the darkness, but shall have the light of life."

Light means Wisdom. It is the Wisdom of this new kind of Life.

You have that new kind of Life.

You have His Wisdom, and that Wisdom gives you the Ability to make the right choices, to do the right thing at the right time.

Not only that, but it gives you the ability to enter into all the fulness and all the blessings, and all the riches of His Redemptive work.

You are outstanding immediately. You are not common.

Now you are revelling in I Cor. 3:21: "For all things are yours," whether the revelation of them came to Paul or to Peter or to John, it doesn't make any difference; they are all yours.

And then another strangely beautiful thing is, "And ye are Christ's."

You see, you belong to Him. He is yours and you are His.

Just as a husband owns the bride, He owns you and it is an ownership of Love.

But that isn't all. 2 Cor. 9:8 ought to thrill our hearts. "And God is able to make all grace abound unto you; that ye, having always all sufficiency in everything, may abound unto every good work."

I wonder if you have read that in Way's translation. "Ay, and God is able to lavish every gracious gift upon you, so that you, always possessing abundance of everything, may lavishly contribute to every good undertaking."

Conybeare translates it, "And God is able to give you an overflowing measure of all good gifts, that all your wants of every kind may be supplied at all times, and you may give of your abundance to every good work."

You see, there is nothing narrow or niggardly in the Father's blessings. There is a wholesome fulness in His blessings.

He has blessed you with every spiritual blessing in Christ.

There isn't a need of yours that hasn't been met.

The Ability of the Father is at your disposal in every crisis of your life, and in your daily life His love so enriches you that there is no wear and tear.

You just pass along on a smooth, easy road, carried by His Grace, upheld by His Love, but His very fulness of Love and Grace overshadow you.

You are rich. You are God's cared-for.

The reason I am writing this is to give you a photograph of what you are in Christ, so that you will rise up and take your place and enjoy the riches that belong to you, and that you will learn to give place to His ability in you.

You will learn to have confidence in the God who is in you.

You will learn to talk about Him as you talk about a strong man that is working for you, or you brag about a car that laughs at hills and mountains.

Why, greater is He that is in you than any mountain, any difficulty, any combination of circumstances.

You are tied up with God.

God is on your side. He is fighting your battles.

All you have to do is just to act on His Word; walk in His Word.

That is His will for you, and you will be amazed how sweet and beautiful life becomes.

You will learn another thing: The authority and power of the Living Word in your lips.

You can say to sickness and disease, "In the Name of Jesus, leave this body," and that Living Word in your lips will be obeyed by the author of sickness and disease.

His Word in your lips puts Him to work at once; gives Him an opportunity to demonstrate His Ability to help man.

His Word in your lips will lead men and women to Christ; will break the power of Satan over the weak.

You will not need another man's faith.

You have passed into the realm of the ones who are not begging for a free ride, but you are able to give a free ride to another.

You have become a dominant spirit rather than a hectored, broken, helpless one.

You have passed out of the realm of liability into God's assets.

You are becoming strong, and you are taking over the weaknesses of others.

You see that brother's overload and you get under it.

You will have a joy that is unspeakable now and full of His glory.

Chapter XVII

THE LIMITATIONS OF JESUS

URING Jesus' earth walk He was dealing exclusively with the Jews – the First Covenant people.

He was surrounded by men who had never been born again.

No person with whom He dealt had yet received Eternal Life. They were all spiritually dead.

John 8:44,45 is Jesus' description of them: "Ye are of your father the devil, and the lusts of your father it is your will to do."

How hard it must have been for the Master, whose great heart of love yearned over the people, to tell them that unhappy truth.

He never conformed Himself to His surroundings or to the opinions of people.

He always spoke out from His Father.

It has been an unhappy thing that so many of our teachers have spoken of those who walked with Jesus, as though they were already Christians, as though they had received Eternal Life.

If anyone could have received Eternal Life before Jesus died and arose again, then He would not have had to suffer, because every one could have received it.

It is not what a man has done; it is what he is by nature that separates him from God. They were all spiritually dead.

Jesus was limited very largely to the physical realm with them.

He healed their diseases; He raised their dead; He fed the multitudes, but He did not Recreate anyone.

He gave no one Eternal Life.

Man was not yet Redeemed; the penalty of sin had not been paid.

Men were by nature children of wrath.

They were all in one class.

The only difference between the Israelite and the Gentile was that the former was under the First Covenant.

He was circumcised; he was of the family of Abraham.

He had a priesthood that made a yearly Atonement for him and laid his sins once a year upon the head of a scape-goat to be borne away into the wilderness.

But that did not make him a New Creation.

It gave him a right to the New Creation.

You remember Rom. 3:25 declares, "Whom God set forth to be a propitiation, through faith, in his blood, to show his righteousness because of the passing over of the sins done aforetime, in the forebearance of God."

Then Heb. 9:15 explains the thing more fully. "For this cause he is a mediator of a new covenant, that a death having taken place for the redemption of the transgressions that were under the First Covenant, they that have been called may receive the promise of the eternal inheritance."

Christ died for the sins of those under the First Covenant.

It was as though a promissory note had been given each year when the High Priest entered the Holy of Holies to make the yearly atonement.

Those promissory notes were all cashed when Jesus carried His blood into the Heavenly Holy of Holies.

So all the sins under the First Covenant were put away, wiped out as though they had never been.

You will understand this more fully in Heb. 10:1-4: "For the law having a shadow of the good things to come, not the very image of the things, can never with the same sacrifices year by year, which they offer continually, make perfect them that draw nigh.

"Else would they not have ceased to be offered? Because the worshippers, having been once cleansed, would have had no more consciousness of sins.

"But in those sacrifices there is a remembrance made of sins year by year."

Why? "For it is impossible that the blood of bulls and goats should take away sins."

(Verse 12) "But he, when he had offered one sacrifice for sins for ever, sat down at the right hand of God."

(Verse 14) "For by one offering he hath perfected for ever them that are sanctified."

You get a perfect picture here of the man under the First Covenant whose sin was covered, whose sins were typically borne away.

Then Jesus comes and puts away all the sin that had been covered and He remits all the sins that have been borne away typically, so that the Jews who trusted in the atoning blood of animals were saved by His sacrifice.

Notice again that no one could receive Eternal Life and have his sins remitted until sin was put away, until the claims of Justice had been fully met.

Heb. 2:17 perfectly illustrates that: "Wherefore it behooved him in all things to be made like unto his brethren, that he might become a merciful and faithful high priest in things pertaining to God, to make propitiation for the sins of the people."

As a High Priest, you remember, He had first to meet the demands of Justice, to satisfy the claims of Justice against the Jew and Gentile.

When He was down in hell and Satan had been conquered, then man's Redemption was a completed thing. That is when God accepted His blood, and He sat down at the right hand of God.

But it was not yet complete while Christ was living, so it was of no value to anybody.

The New Creation was not available.

There was no High Priest at the right hand of the Father with the blood to show that He had dealt with the sin problem.

There was no Mediator at the right hand of God, and until there was a Mediator, no human being could approach God.

John 14:6, "I am the way, the truth and the life; no one can approach the Father but through me."

Acts 4:12, "Neither is there any other name under heaven, that is given among men, wherein we must be saved, but the name of Jesus."

Jesus' name was not yet available as a Savior.

His Mediatorial work was not yet available.

Jesus was a prophet now. He had not yet become a Sin Substitute; there was no Savior.

He dealt only in the sense realm with men.

He dealt with demons.

He cast them out of individuals.

He broke their power over men, which was all in the sense realm.

It is such a bitter thing for our hearts to realize that Jesus, during His earth walk, didn't have one single spiritually-minded companion.

Good folks loved Him, but their love was the love of natural man.

It was a selfish thing. It was so selfish that when He arose from the dead they said, "Master, are you going to restore the kingdom at this time?"

He could not help men spiritually because they were dead in spirit.

I think you can understand this Scripture now: John 14:12 "Greater things than these shall ye do; because I go unto the Father and ye behold me no more."

We are doing greater works than the Master did in His earth walk, because we help men spiritually.

111

We bring to them the Word of Life and they are Recreated; they come into the Family of God.

We help them to pass out of death unto Life.

We teach them through the Word how God has made them His Righteousness.

Now they can stand in His presence as though sin had never been.

We are God's agents giving men Eternal Life, making them masters of demons and of circumstances.

We, through His Living Word, have been able to lead men into fellowship and communion with the Father through the New Birth.

Our ministry is almost an unlimited ministry.

His Ministry was a limited one.

Jesus healed men's bodies.

We, through the Grace of God, heal men's spirits.

He raised men from the dead to die again.

We show them that they were raised together with Christ.

He fed the hungry with loaves of bread and fishes.

We feed the spiritually hungry with His own wonderful Words.

We have the Spirit in us who raised Jesus from the dead.

We have a legal right to the use of Jesus' name.

With that name we do the works that Jesus wrought in His earth walk.

But come back again to the thought of the limitations of Jesus' friendships.

His own Mother could not understand Him. His own brothers looked upon Him with suspicion.

To those nearest Him He was a stranger. He knew them but they didn't know Him.

There can be no deep spiritual friendship unless we know each other.

Jesus' limitations in His earth walk explain much of His teaching.

It might be all right for us to contrast Jesus' and Paul's teachings on the subject of Faith.

Jesus demanded that men have faith in Him. He said, "if a man have faith as a mustard seed, he could move mountains."

In Mark 11:22 Jesus said, "Have faith in God.'"

You remember in the margin of some of our Bibles it says, "Have the faith of God."

The disciples couldn't do that.

No one can have the Faith of God until after they have been Re-created.

You see, Jesus is the author and finisher of faith, and when we become New Creations we receive a measure of God's Faith. (Rom. 12:3).

We have His Nature, His Life, and with it comes His Faith.

As we grow in Grace and in Knowledge, we understand the finished work of Christ. As our faith grows, it is really the Faith of God.

In the next verse it says, "Verily I say unto you, Whosoever shall say unto this mountain, Be thou taken up and cast into the sea; and shall not doubt in his heart, but shall believe that what he saith cometh to pass; he shall have it.

"Therefore I say unto you, All things whatsoever ye pray and ask for, believe that ye receive them, and ye shall have them."

That was a keynote of the ministry of Jesus.

Mark 9:23, Jesus said to the father that asked for the healing of his child, "All things are possible to him that believeth."

In Matt. 21:22 "And all things, whatsoever ye shall ask in prayer, believing, ye shall receive."

Paul never tells a believer to believe.

He never urges us to have Faith.

That bothered me when I first noticed it; then I saw the truth.

We are believers.

We had to have faith to get into the Family, but when once we come into the Family, all things that God wrought in Christ for us are ours.

You notice Jesus, speaking to the Church prophetically, (for the Church had not yet come into being) said in John 15:16, "Ye did not choose me, but I chose you, and appointed you, that ye should go and bear fruit, and that your fruit should abide; that whatsoever ye shall ask of the Father in my name, he may give it you."

In this Scripture and John 14:14 Jesus gives us a legal right to the use of His Name.

It is the same as giving the power of attorney to one.

Jesus actually does this to the Church.

But here is the strange thing about it. Take John 16:24 "Hitherto have ye asked nothing in my name: ask, and ye shall receive, that your joy may be made full." (John 15:16 is Prophecy.)

Jesus doesn't mention faith. He doesn't say that they must believe.

Why? They are believers.

Then all of our preaching about faith and the need of faith has been wrong.

We should have told the believer about what he is in Christ; what his rights and privileges are in Christ and his legal right to the use of Jesus' name.

We should have taught him what it meant to receive the Nature and Life of God in his spirit, that it would make him an actual New Creation.

Not only that, but the New Creation had become the Righteousness of God in Christ, so he who was once a sinner could now stand in the Father's presence without the sense of fear, condemnation or inferiority.

He could stand there as a Son in fullest fellowship with his Father.

If we had been taught this, we would not have had the long struggle for faith.

We would have known who we were and what we were in Christ.

We would have learned how to take our place in the Family; how to enjoy our privileges.

We would have become acquainted with our Father.

The great facts of Substitution and the New Creation and Redemption would have become spiritual realities to us.

But instead of that, they have preached to us the messages Jesus gave to the Jews during His earth walk, and they don't fit in.

They keep us under condemnation. They make us conscious of our lack.

You see, if I do not know what I am, the Word confuses me, but when I know what I am in Christ, know what my rights are and my privileges, then you can bring no confusion to my spirit.

There was no discord between the teachings of Jesus and the Apostle Paul because they were all of God.

Chapter XVIII

THE DEFEATED SATAN

EW of us have ever recognized the fact that the Scriptures teach that Satan is defeated as far as the believer is concerned.

He was not conquered by the believer; he was conquered by Christ for the believer in His Substitutionary Work.

The victory Christ wrought belongs to the believer, because we were identified with Christ in His Substitutionary Work.

We have mentioned this in another chapter, but I wish to go a little farther with you in this.

In Gal. 2:20 Paul cries, "I have been crucified with Christ." Not "I am" as the old version gives it.

Back yonder when Christ hung on the cross, in the mind of Justice, every one of us hung there.

We were identified with Him because He was our Substitute.

He was taking our place in order that He might redeem us out of the hand of our enemy.

We were with Him when He died, for we died with Him.

We were with Him when He left His body.

We were with Him in His great agony, while He suffered the penalty that was due us.

He was in the prison house of death. Satan was its keeper.

The horror of it will never be known.

Jesus stayed there until He satisfied the claims of Justice for us.

Rom. 4:25 says, "Who was delivered up on account of our trespasses," that is, He was delivered up to death, spiritual death.

He was delivered up to judgment. He was delivered up to pay the penalty that we owed Justice, and when the claims of Justice were satisfied, then we were justified with Christ.

That is the reason every unsaved man has a legal right to Eternal Life, because he was legally Justified with Christ in that great Substitutionary work.

Then Jesus was Born Again. You remember the Scripture in Acts 13:33, "Thou art my Son, this day have I begotten thee," that was the day of our Redemption.

I want to pause here just a bit and call your attention to a startling fact.

You remember when Jesus entered the Holy of Holies with His

blood, He had just come out of hell, and when the Father justified Him, He was so Justified that He could stand in the Father's presence without the slightest bit of condemnation.

Like the three Hebrew children, when they came out of the fiery furnace there was no smell of fire upon their garments.

There was no smell on the garments of our Lord.

Do you know what that shows me? If Jesus could go out of there and go into the presence of the Father, you and I can go out of this world ruled by spiritual death.

We who have received Eternal Life, can go into the presence of the Father without the sense or the smell of spiritual death upon us.

As soon as the Master was made alive in spirit, then Col. 2:15 became a Reality. "Having put off from himself the principalities and the powers, he made a show of them openly."

Right there in the presence of all the hosts of darkness, Jesus conquered the Prince of Darkness.

Heb. 2:14 in Rotherham's Translation is graphic: "He paralyzed the death-dealing power of Satan." He paralyzed him. He broke him.

Now this is what I want you to notice: This was an eternal victory. Satan was eternally broken, eternally conquered.

Did you notice how Peter puts it? 1 Pet. 5:8, "He goes about like a roaring lion," and he says, "Whom withstand steadfast in your faith."

Our combat has been fought and won.

There isn't any battle for you to fight except the battle of faith.

You are to fight the good fight of faith.

What does that mean? You are to win all your victories with words.

You are to learn the words of this Wonderful Book, and with words you will conquer your enemy.

All that Peter said to the sick man at the Beautiful Gate was, "In the name of Jesus Christ of Nazareth, rise and walk," and the man was set free. (Acts 3:1-11).

He didn't lay hands on him. He didn't pray over him. He simply healed that man with words.

That is the way Jesus healed them – with words.

That is the way the Father created the Universe – with words.

You conquer the adversary with words.

Today you comfort the weak and the broken with words.

You heal the sick with words.

Why, when I read Isa. 53:4, "Surely he hath borne my sicknesses, and carried my diseases, and I have come to esteem him as the one who was stricken, smitten of God, and afflicted with my diseases," then I knew that by His stripes I was healed.

What healed me? Words.

Now you can understand Psa. 107:20, "He sent his word, and healed them."

It isn't prayer. It isn't laying on of our hands.

That may be necessary among the babes in Christ, but for the man that is grown up into the full stature of the knowledge of his rights and privileges, the Word heals him.

The Word brought that money to me. I had called my Father's attention to Phil. 4:19, "My God shall supply every need of yours" and He did it, "according to His riches in glory in Christ Jesus."

That settled it. His Words brought comfort and assurance to me. Then I simply said, "In the name of Jesus, you ministering spirits, go and cause that money to come," and the money came. Not once, but it has been coming all these years of my public ministry.

You see, our combat is not against flesh and blood, as the Spirit tells us in Eph. 6:12, but it is against the defeated principalities and powers.

These principalities and powers have all been conquered.

Their defeat is spoken of in Heb. 9:12 as an eternal redemption from them.

You are eternally set free.

They are eternally defeated, whipped, conquered.

You get your liberty by remembering these words and then acting accordingly.

You simply refuse to stay in bondage.

With joy you read this Scripture: "In whom I have my redemption through His blood, the remission of my trespasses, according to the riches of His grace." (Eph. 1:6).

Can't you see what it means? That Satan knows he is whipped but he doesn't want you to know it.

He wants to keep you in ignorance of it.

Rev. 12:11 has been a source of great comfort to me: "And they overcame him because of the blood of the Lamb and the word of their testimony."

That Word is Logos. In the beginning was the Logos, and the Logos was with God, and the Logos was God."

Can't you see, they overcame him with the Word of Christ. That meant they overcame him with Christ Himself.

That blood is the basis, the ground of our victory.

It proves to all Heaven that Satan was defeated, and I act on the ground of that.

Now I shout! If He is for me (and He is for me), then who is there in earth or hell that can stand up against me!

I am a conqueror!

As a nation, we are facing one of the gravest periods of our national life, and it is necessary that there arise a company of men and women who know the power of the Name of Jesus and how to use that Name against our national enemies.

Our worst enemy is not a foreign enemy. It is a local enemy. It is in our midst.

Now you are to rise up and to use His words, these demon-destroying words; these demon-defeating words; these circumstance-defeating words.

When you go into the Throne Room, you talk to the Father; you are taking into His presence His own Word.

Jesus no more spoke the Word of the Father than you, if you will use His Word now.

The Father shows respect always to His Own Word. He says, "I watch over my word to perform it." "No word from me will ever be void of power (or fulfillment)." (Luke 1:37).

Go in there then and lay your request upon that Word.

I like to think that I lay them upon the Name of Jesus, and I hold that Name up before Him with my request upon it.

"Whatsoever ye shall ask of the Father in my name, he will give it you." (John 15:15).

We are living in this Living Truth.

We are taking advantage of its mighty possibilities, and we are daring to pray; we are daring to face the hosts of darkness with a consciousness that our prayers will be answered, and that the forces of darkness are beaten and defeated.

We no longer hold them as doctrines; they are a part of us.

We live these words and they live in us.

John 15:7 declares, "If ye abide in me and my words are living in you, ye shall demand your rights and they shall be rendered to you. The Father will bring those things to pass Himself.

You understand you didn't choose Him, but He chose you, and He told you to go and bear fruit.

That will be Word fruit; Prayer fruit.

We have reached the place where we need to change the minds of men and women around us.

There is a spiritual sense of defeat in the hearts of the great masses in the Church.

This has been brought about by the liquor traffic, by the open saloons, by the girls sitting at the bar.

Prostitution and delinquency have run riot with it.

The rebellion of the teen age youth against parental instruction and their absence from the church has broken like a running sore in the heart of the nation.

But has God gone out of business? Has He lost His Ability?

Look at the heathen world the little Church faced.

Look at the educational skepticism in the Jewish nation.

Look at the whole black picture of the Roman Empire.

The Church sent out uneducated, untrained men to face that awful condition and carve new nations out of it. They won, and we can win.

We must check off the world's mental influence.

We must take our place and shout aloud, "We are what He says we are."

We can do what He says we can do.

We are linked with God by His Nature. There is a human-divine union between the Eternal Father and the believer.

Our spirits have the creative energy and ability that is in the Father's Spirit.

We are meeting conditions as conquerors.

His Word in our lips can defeat any force or element that comes against us.

By His All-powerful Name we go against these problems and conquer them.

I can hear Him whisper, "Lo, I am with you; go ahead, I will see you through. I will be with you."

Once again I hear that song of triumph of the ages: "Fear thou not, for I am with thee; be not dismayed, for I am thy God." (Isa. 41:10).

"The God who opened the Red Sea, who destroyed the power of the flames when those three Hebrew boys were thrown into the fiery furnace is with you.

"I am the God of all ages.

"Lo, I am with you: all my forces are for you, and you are a victor in the face of all your enemies."

119

Chapter XIX

THE END OF CONDEMNATION

HE title to this chapter would likely have confused some of us a few years ago, because all we had ever heard was condemnation.

Most of our great evangelists have been preachers of Condemnation, preachers of Judgment.

Few of them have ever revealed to us what we were in Christ. They have magnified sin above Redemption.

Rom. 8:1 has been almost an unknown Scripture: "There is therefore now no condemnation to them that are in Christ Jesus."

If we had known that we could stand before the Father just as freely as Adam did in the Garden, as Jesus did in His earth walk, it would have made life a great deal different.

This struggle after faith was because of a sense of unworthiness on our part.

We have had the sense of unrighteousness built into us by our teachers. We have not known what Redemption means to the believer.

2 Cor. 5:17-21 contains the story of the New Creation and of man's standing before the Father:

"Wherefore if any man is in Christ, there is a New Creation (a new species): the old things are passed away; behold, they are become new. But all these things are of God, who reconciled us to himself through Christ, and gave unto us the ministry of reconciliation."

The old things of condemnation, the old things of sin and weakness, of failure, of doubt and fear are passed away, and there has come into us a New Creation without condemnation, without fear.

We have become instantaneously a child of God and we are reconciled to Him.

There is no condemnation, there is no fear, there is no sense of sin or of unworthiness.

Like a child in its Mother's bosom, we are perfectly restful and contented.

Not only that, "But he has given unto us a ministry of reconciliation, to-wit, that God was in Christ reconciling the world to himself, not reckoning unto them their trespasses, and having committed unto us the word of reconciliation." (Verse 19).

120

We have followed in the path of our forefathers who had developed in themselves a sense of unworthiness and sin, so that whenever they prayed they had to ask for forgiveness and cry for mercy.

They acted as though they had never been Born Again, as though sin had never been put away, and that the Father looked upon them with suspicion and doubt.

But did you notice that 19th verse? He is not even reckoning the sinners their sins, because He laid their sins on Christ.

Why should he reckon unto us, His own Sons and Daughters in Christ, a sin-consciousness?

He has not.

We have built it into ourselves through our ignorance.

Our sins have been wiped out as though they had never been.

That old wicked self has been put away and a New Self has taken its place.

We are New Creations.

Then in the 21st verse he says these marvelous words: "Him who knew no sin he made to be sin on our behalf; that we might become the righteousness of God in Him."

And the next verse, did you notice it? "And working together with him we entreat also that ye receive not the grace of God in vain."

You couldn't work together with Him unless you were Righteous, unless you were in fellowship with Him.

He has made you by the New Birth, the very Righteousness of God in Christ.

The sin problem is settled for the believer.

Now it is the problem of my entering into my inheritance.

You see, I shared with Him in His death.

I shared with Him in His suffering.

I shared with Him when He was made Righteous.

I shared with Him when He was made alive.

I shared with Him when He met the adversary in the dark regions and conquered him.

I shared with Him when he arose from the dead.

I shared with Him in the mind of Justice when He sat down at the right hand of the Majesty on High.

I am seated there according to His own Word.

I am free from condemnation.

I am free from the guilt of my old conduct and my union with Satan.

I turn to Rom. 8:31 and I read what He inspired Paul to write for me. "What then shall I say to these things? If God is for me, who is against me."

That settles it. I can hear Him whisper, "He that spared not His own Son, but delivered him up for us all, how shall he not also with him freely give us all things."

And then He says these marvelous words: "Who shall lay anything to the charge of God's elect? It is God that justifieth."

"Who is He that has the ability to condemn? It is Christ Jesus that died, yea rather, that was raised from the dead, who is at the right hand of God, who also maketh intercession for us."

Then he asks this burning question: "Who shall separate us from the love of Christ? shall tribulation, or anguish, or persecution, or famine, or nakedness, or peril, or sword?"

None of these things can bring the believer under condemnation.

I wonder if you have read Eph. 1:5-7 carefully: "Having marked us out for the position of sons through Jesus Christ unto himself. He did this according to the good pleasure of his will, to the praise of the glory of his grace which he freely bestowed on us in the beloved."

Where are you? You are in the Beloved.

That means that you are beloved; that you are a part of the Beloved.

You are identified with Him; you are one with Him.

In the 7th verse it says, we have been redeemed through His blood. We received "the remission of our trespasses, and it was according to the riches of His grace which he made to abound toward us in all wisdom and prudence."

There is no place for condemnation.

The only problem is this: Have we learned how to walk in fellowship with Him?

Have we learned how to maintain our fellowship?

This law is laid down in the Pauline Revelation and in John's wonderful epistles.

We must walk in Love as Jesus walked in Love.

But you say, "How can I do it?"

You have received the Love Nature of the Father, haven't you?

You have become a partaker of the Divine Nature. That is Love. "God is Love."

Then learn to let that Love Nature dominate you.

Paul said he kept his body under. He meant, he kept his senses from dominating him.

As far as the believer is concerned, selfishness emanates from the senses.

Then if you keep the senses in subjection, give Love the right of way, you will walk in fellowship with Him.

I John 1:3-5 "That which we have seen and heard declare we unto you also, that ye also may have fellowship with us: yea, and our fellowship is with the Father, and with his Son Jesus Christ. These things we write, that your joy may be made full.

"And this is the message which we have heard from him and announce unto you, that God is light, and in him is no darkness at all. If we say that we have fellowship with him and walk in the darkness, we lie, and do not the truth."

What does that mean? If I step out of Love, I step out of Light into darkness. When I step into darkness I know not where I am going.

I John 2:10,11 tells us, "He that loveth his brother abideth in the light, and there is no occasion of stumbling in him. But he that hateth his brother is in the darkness, and knoweth not whither he goeth, because the darkness hath blinded his eyes."

If we break fellowship, I John 1:9 tells how to have it restored. "If we confess our sins (things we have done that brought us into darkness), he is faithful and righteous to forgive us our sins, and to cleanse us from all unrighteousness."

Now you can see that as far as you are concerned as a New Creation, you have reached the end of condemnation.

It is not necessary to live in it another day.

The Son has made you free.

Now live and walk in that freedom.

Chapter XX

WALKING AS MERE MEN

NE of the saddest facts that we have to face today is that the Sons of God, men with God in them, men with the very Nature of God, are walking "as mere men of the world."

Hear Weymouth's Translation of I Cor. 3:1-4: "And as for myself, brethren, I found it impossible to speak to you as spiritual men. It had to be as to worldlings – mere babes in Christ.

"I fed you with milk and not with solid food, since for this you were not yet strong enough. And even now you are not strong enough: you are still unspiritual.

"For so long as jealousy and strife continue among you, can it be denied that you are unspiritual and are living and acting like mere men of the world? For when some one says, 'I belong to Paul,' and another says, 'I belong to Apollos,' is not this the way men of the world speak?"

Paul found it impossible to write about the deeply spiritual aspect of Christ's Substitution.

He found it impossible to write to them about the New Creation because they lived in the realm of the senses.

They had never developed their Recreated Spirit.

You see, the believer, when born into the Family, has a measure of Faith, has a measure of Love; the Love of God is shed abroad in his heart by the Holy Spirit.

But unless he grows in Grace and in the knowledge of the Lord Jesus Christ, unless he studies to show himself approved unto the Father, he remains unspiritual.

His spirit is never cultivated, never developed.

You can develop your spirit as you can develop your mind, as you can develop your physical muscles.

The average believer has never developed his spirit. Consequently his Faith is weak, his Love is weak, and his Knowledge is often mixed with error.

You must remember that Love does not come from the reasoning faculties; neither does Faith.

Faith and Love are both born in the Recreated human spirit.

The reason Jesus said in Matt. 4:4 "Man shall not live by bread alone, but by every word that proceedeth out of the mouth of God," was not to cultivate man's intellectual and reasoning faculties, but to cultivate his spirit.

In Eph. 1:17,18 Paul had prayed that the "Father of glory, may give unto you a spirit of wisdom and revelation in the knowledge of him; having the eyes of your heart enlightened."

The heart is called in Rom. 7:22, "The inward man."

In I Pet. 3:4 it is "The hidden man of the heart."

You see, man is a spirit being and the part of him that is spiritually dead is his spirit.

After he is Recreated, then his spirit must be educated, trained and developed.

As the spirit grows strong and vigorous in the Word, Faith becomes strong and Love becomes like the Master's Love.

As long as we walk in the senses and follow the inclinations of the senses, the spirit is not developed and we are walking as mere men.

We walk as though we had never received Eternal Life.

The believer has limitless possibilities in this Divine Life.

Eph. 1:3 gives us a picture of the developed Recreated spirit. It says, "Who hath blessed us with every spiritual blessing in the heavenlies."

If we have those blessings, then the unsearchable riches of Christ really belong to us.

In Eph. 3:8 Paul says he preached unto the Gentiles the unsearchable riches of Christ.

In Eph. 3:12 he says, "In whom we have boldness and access in confidence through our faith in him."

There is no limit to this New Life.

He says in Eph. 4:7, "Unto each one of us was the grace given according to the measure of the gift of Christ."

And in Eph. 4:1 he said, "I, therefore, the prisoner in the Lord, beseech you to walk worthy of the calling wherewith ye were called."

We are to walk in Love; to walk in the fulness of His fellowship.

We are to grow in Grace and in the knowledge of it "till we all attain to the unity of faith, and of the knowledge of the Son of God, unto a full grown man, unto the measure of the stature of the fulness of Christ" (Eph. 4:13).

He doesn't want us to be "any longer children tossed to and fro and tossed about by every wind of doctrine."

He wants us to grow up into the full stature of the Jesus Life.

It belongs to us.

You can understand that you have become a partaker of the very Nature of the Father, and that everything Jesus purchased for you in His Redemptive work is available to you.

There is no ground for a man to be weak.

There is no ground for a man to be always talking about his lack of faith and lack of this or that, "for of His fulness have we all received, and grace upon grace."

In the mind of the Father you are complete in Him, who is the Head of all principality and power.;

You are complete in His completeness.

I shall never forget the thrill that Eph. 1:22,23 gave to my heart: "And he put all things in subjection under his feet, and gave him to be head over all things to the church, which is his body, the fulness of him that filleth all in all."

We are the Body; we are the feet of Christ.

We are the part of the Body that is running errands for the Master, and He has put all the forces of darkness under our feet.

One of us could chase a thousand, and two could put ten thousand to flight.

The ability of God that is within us is utterly limitless.

What are we going to do with a Scripture like this: 2 Cor. 3:4,5, "And such confidence have we through Christ to Godward; not that we are sufficient of ourselves, to account anything as from ourselves; but our sufficiency is from God."

"Who made us sufficient as ministers of a New Covenant." That doesn't mean preachers only; that means everyone of us.

We have His sufficiency; we have His ability.

How it staggers one when we get the right translation of Luke 24:49, "But tarry in the city, until ye be clothed with power from on high."

This was Jesus' message to the disciples before He ascended. He wanted them clothed with power. The correct word for power means "ability."

Now He says, "I want you clothed with ability from on high," the Father's ability.

You can hear Him say, "Now you will be able to understand the messages that I have given to you.

"You will have ability to know what the New Creation means.

"You will have ability to enter into the fulness of this Divine Life.

"You will have ability to be my witness, to heal the sick, to cast out demons, and to use my Name against all the forces of darkness."

You will know what Mark 16:17 means where He says, "In my name ye shall cast out demons."

Also, John 16:23 "Whatsoever ye shall ask the Father in my name, he will give it you."

You see, until our hearts take in these truths, we are going to walk "as mere men."

You remember Sampson, that mighty Covenant man.

There never was a man like him, and yet when he ignored his Covenant rights, the Philistines captured him and put out his eyes and made a slave of him.

The eyes of the heart of most believers are like Sampson's eyes. They have lost their ability to enjoy the fulness of their rights in Christ.

John 10:29 has never meant anything to many of them. Let me read it to you: "My Father, who hath given them unto me, is greater than all; and no one is able to snatch them out of the Father's hand. I and the Father are one."

They have never learned to say,

> My Father is greater than all;
> My Father is greater than all.
> 'Mid life's bitter tears,
> Temptations and fears,
> My Father is greater than all.

They have never realized they had a Father. He has only been God to them.

They have never whispered, "My Father, I love you."

The Father has never been able to make Himself real to their hearts because sense knowledge has so completely governed them.

He is a Father God and He Loves you.

Heb. 7:25 has never been in the background of their consciousness as a great living force: "Wherefore also he is able to save to the uttermost them that draw near unto God through him, seeing he ever liveth to make intercession for them."

The harder circumstances may press upon you, the more fully does He uphold you.

His intercession for you means there isn't power enough in the world to take you captive if you are in fellowship with the Father.

He ever lives for your benefit. He loves you.

He gave Himself up for you. He is longing for you to respond to that Love.

He is longing for you to look up and whisper, " Jesus, I love you."

Redemption Minded

The Father would like you to become Redemption-minded.

I do not see how you can act as "a mere man" any longer.

Don't cause His heart to ache over you because you have become circumstance-minded, sickness-minded, failure-minded.

He never created a failure; He made us for victory.

You have the use of Jesus' Name. Use it. It gives you access into the Father's very presence.

It gives you victory over disease, over circumstances, over the forces of darkness.

You have the same great Mighty Holy Spirit that Jesus and the Apostles had in their walk.

Jesus is your Wisdom.

He is today the very strength of your life.

You are now blessed with every spiritual blessing.

You don't need to cry for faith, nor pray for strength.

You have it all; it belongs to you.

You have been blessed with everything that Redemption could give.

I would that you might become so conscious of the presence of the Master, that "Lo, I am with you alway" will become just an unconscious fact, so that no matter what happens, you know He is there.

"Forgetteth What Manner of Man He Was"

James is describing the "doer of the Word." He is more than a teacher of the Word.

He is more than an admirer of the Word.

He is more than a student of the Word.

The Word is living in him.

He is living so that Word is a part of his very being.

He walks in Love. His whole conduct is governed by the New Law of the New Creation.

He doesn't permit his lips to sin against his spirit.

He has learned to weigh carefully the value of words.

So James 1:22-25 has become a very serious section of the Word to him. "Be ye doers of the word, and not hearers only, deluding your own selves."

How many good people have deluded themselves.

They believe in the teachings of their Church.

They don't study the Word much.

128

They are very careful about what man says and often deny themselves much and put themselves under bondage because of man's word.

James is bringing us face to face with the Father himself. He says, "Be ye doers of the word," and so I study the Word to find out what it says and then I do it.

The Love Law was given to govern our conduct toward each other, and so I study it diligently.

"For if any one is a hearer of the word and not a doer, he is like unto a man beholding his natural face in a mirror: for he beholdeth himself, and goeth away, and straightway forgetteth what manner of man he was." (Jas. 1:23, 24).

Let us see what manner of men we are, what the Father says about us.

We should take account of stock and find what we are in the mind of the Father.

Rom. 8:14-16, "For as many as are led by the Spirit of God, these are sons of God," or they become sons of God.

If a man is willing to be led by the Spirit, he will be led into Sonship.

"For ye received not the spirit of bondage again unto fear; but ye received the spirit of adoption, whereby we cry, Abba, Father. The Spirit himself beareth witness with our spirit, that we are children of God: and if children, then heirs; heirs of God, and joint-heirs with Christ."

That is what the Father says we are.

We are in His family; a part of the Body of Christ.

We are what the Spirit calls the New Creation man.

We have passed out of the realm of satanic relationship into the Family of the Father God.

Col. 1:13 tells us that "we have been translated out of the kingdom of darkness into the kingdom of the Son of his love."

If that is true (and it *is* true), then we are a new type, a new class of men.

We should study the Word that we might know what the Father expects of us and what the world has a right to expect from us.

We are a supernatural people.

We have the ability of God, the wisdom of God. We have the mind of God in His Word.

We should never forget "what manner of men we are."

No matter what the crisis may be; no matter what testings may come to us, we do not forget what manner of men we are.

You see, we belong to a new order.

We belong to the class of people that have a legal right to enter the Father's presence anytime, anywhere.

Not only have we a right, but we have a standing invitation to come boldly to the Throne of Grace.

We are the Righteous men.

We have been made Righteous by the Nature of the Father that was imparted to us when we became New Creations.

That Righteousness of God makes us masters of every force outside of God.

We are in league with Heaven and have the backing of Heaven.

We can hear Paul saying, "If God is for us, who can be against us."

He is for us: He is on our side.

In Rom. 8:31-39 He goes over all of the forces that may antagonize us, that may come against us, and He shows us that we can be masters of everything that Satan can possibly bring against us.

There isn't a weapon that Satan has, but what we are proof against it.

You see, our combat is not with flesh and blood; it is not with sense knowledge things; it is with spiritual forces, and in all these things we are more than masters.

They cannot separate us from the Love of God that is in Christ Jesus.

If they could separate us from His Love, they could defeat us; but He loves us and it causes Him to succor us, care for us, watch over us, shield us.

We must not forget for one moment that the great Mighty Spirit who raised Jesus from the dead, the Person who gave to the world its vegetation, that Mighty One, is living in us, for it is God who is at work within us willing and working His own good pleasure.

If one accustomed themselves to trust in Him as we trust in the money that is in our pocket–book, as we trust in our car when it is filled with oil and gas, what mighty men and women would walk the earth.

The Father would be so real to them; the Name would be so real; there would be a consciousness of the fact that Jesus said, "All authority has been given unto me in heaven and on earth."

"Go ye, therefore, as my representatives. I will give you a legal right to the use of my Name. In my Name you are the master of demons, of diseases, of the laws of nature that would in any wise hinder you from doing my will."

You see, we are empowered representatives of the Heavenly Kingdom.

We should never forget what manner of men we are.

We send our Ambassador to England.

He must never forget that he is not a mere man now. He is a representative of our Government.

Our Government is behind him.

He is saying the words that our Government has instructed him to say.

He is not acting on his own initiative. He is not a mere man.

He is an Ambassador on the behalf of our Government.

I must not forget what manner of man I am.

I am an Ambassador on behalf of Christ. As an Ambassador, I have the backing of the Supreme Court of the Universe.

I have the backing of my Father God, of Jesus, of the great mighty Holy Spirit, and all the angels of God.

You see, I can't be a failure unless I forget what manner of man. I am.

I don't know whether you ever noticed I Cor. 3:1-3: "And I, brethren, could not speak unto you as unto spiritual, but as unto carnal, as unto babes in Christ."

It is just as though he said, "I wish I could speak to you as to men who realized who they were, what they were, and what they could do, but I cannot because you are living in the sense realm."

You have no confidence in the great spiritual realities to which you are united.

You are living just like babes.

You don't seem to grasp the reality of your unity with Deity.

Paul cries, "I fed you with milk, not with meat; for ye were not yet able to bear it: nay, not even now are ye able."

What a pathetic confession.

What a humiliating confession, when by reason of time they ought to take advantage of what they were in Christ but they haven't done it.

They have been content to listen to the voices of men, to read the literature of men, but have ignored the literature of Heaven, the voice of Him who raised Jesus from the dead.

The next verse throws light on it. He said, "For ye are yet sense ruled: for whereas there is among you all the conduct of mere babes in Christ, and you are walking after the manner of men."

Or, as another puts it, "Your conduct is the conduct of mere men when you might walk as the Sons of God."

You might be masters instead of slaves.

Everyone of you could be a leader. Instead of that, you are being led, but not led by God. You are led by sense knowledge, consequently your whole life is disfigured.

You have lost the consciousness of being what you are, and when sickness comes you are in a quandary; you don't know what to do; your heart is filled with fear.

You have never taken your place in Christ.

You have never taken advantage of your rights and privileges in Christ.

You have never asserted your rights as a son in the family.

You have unconsciously relegated yourself to the place of a servant.

You are depending upon other people, and when the problem of faith comes, you talk about your unbelief and your lack.

You are a spiritual hitch-hiker. You have the ability of God, but you do not use it.

You have this Living Word of God.

You are eligible to take advantage of all the privileges that belong to the Sons of God, and yet you are living as a mere man.

You have forgotten what manner of man you are.

Heb. 5:12-14 describes this type of believer. "And when by reason of time you ought to be teachers, ye have need again that some one teach you the rudiments of the first principles of the oracles of God; and are become such as have need of milk, and not of solid food."

This is plain speaking. It is the heart of the Father reaching out to his careless, thoughtless children, and He says, "You had plenty of time.

"You could have taken courses in the study of the Word.

"It wouldn't be necessary for you to go away to a Bible School; you could have correspondence courses.

"You could attend Bible classes very likely in your own church or in your own community.

"You have even forgotten the teachings, the first principles of the New Creation.

"You have forgotten that you have passed out of death unto Life.

"You have forgotten that you are a New Creation created in Christ Jesus.

"You have forgotten that you are tied up with God, that you are a partaker of the Divine Nature.

"You have forgotten that you have within you the very Life of God Himself, and you have at your side the great Paraclete, the Comforter, the Holy Spirit."

He is ready to come in and take possession of you and to be your Teacher and your Guide and your Comforter.

It has been easier for you to read about the Bible than it has to become a student of the Bible and to study to show yourself approved unto God in this Living Word.

You have reached a place where you have need of milk. You need baby treatment and baby care. That is an unhappy thing.

And then He says, "For everyone that partaketh of milk, is inexperienced in the Word that teaches about your righteousness."

You have never exercised yourself to discern between good and evil. That doesn't mean between sin and Rightousness, but between the forces of God and the evil forces that may come disguised to you.

You have lived on the borderland between right and wrong.

You have been asking yourself, is it wrong to do this? Should I do that? These are questions of the babe in Christ.

There has been no growth, no development, and if anyone should say, "Are you a believer?" it is likely you would answer, "Well, I am trying to be."

You see, there isn't any such thing as a believer trying to be a believer, any more than for a boy to try to be a boy. He is a boy. He may decide to be a better boy.

If you say you are trying to be a believer, then you are not a believer. You are outside.

You have never received Eternal Life.

Your spirit has never been Recreated.

So it is vitally important that you study the Word to find what manner of man you are, how the Father looks upon you, and what He expects from you.

Chapter XXI

BELIEVING IN HIS SUBSTITUTION

HEN we use the fact of His Substitution as we use a bridge, or an elevator, then the Word becomes a Reality.

We never think of faith when we take an elevator or train. We simply use them.

If we were New Creation-conscious, as conscious of the fact that we are a New Creation and have the Nature and Life of the Father in us, as we are of the things of the senses, then we would walk in the realm of victory.

You cannot be God-inside-conscious without being a victor. Then I John 4:4 becomes a reality. Notice it now: "Ye are of God, my little children." Let that soak into your spirit consciousness.

Say over and over again, "I am of God; I am born from above; I am born of God; I am a New Creation created in Christ Jesus. I am a master of everything connected with the old creation.

"Satan has no dominion over the New Creation. He has no dominion over me.

"That hidden man of the heart, my spirit, the real me, is a New Creation. The old things have passed away."

The old man with its weaknesses, its failings, its doubts, its fears, its sense of servitude to circumstances, is all gone, and the new spirit, the New Man in Christ, is now a Master where the other was a slave.

This New Creation is redeemed out of the hands of its enemies.

I can hear Paul whisper, "In whom I have my redemption."

You see, that truth is becoming a Reality.

Now I can understand the next sentence in I John 4:4, "For greater is he that is in you than he that is in the world."

I have the Life and Nature of God in me. That makes me a New Creation.

I have invited the One who raised Jesus from the dead, to make His home in me, and He is there.

When I start to study the Word, I always call His attention to it.

When I am to dictate or to preach, I say, "Holy Spirit, here is your opportunity. Now speak through me; think through me; live big in me. Unveil Jesus through these lips."

You see, that great Substitution is ours. He is ours. His Ability is ours.

All that He did is ours, just as our hands and feet are ours.

We look at ourselves now as a New Creation.

We have been taken out of the realm of death as really as Jesus was when He was raised from the dead.

His body was taken out of the realm of physical death; our spirits have been taken out of the realm of spiritual death.

In the mind of Justice, we were raised together with Him.

In reality, when we became New Creations, we passed out of death into Life.

We left the realm of spiritual death.

We left the dominion of death, the family of Satan.

John 5:24 has become a reality. "He that heareth my word, and believeth him that sent me, hath eternal life, and cometh not into judgment, but hath passed out of death into life."

You see, we were born out of spiritual death into the realm of Spiritual Life.

We passed out from Satan's authority and dominion, and have been translated into the kingdom of the Son of His Love, in whom we have our Redemption, the remission of our trespasses.

It is a Redemption that is according to the riches of His Grace, His Love, His Ability.

We have actually passed into the very Family of God.

God is now our Father.

We are His very children.

When that thing happened, we were looked upon as the Sons of God in liberty. For Christ had made us free.

Jesus had become our Righteousness.

By the New Birth, we became partakers of the Divine Nature; we became the Righteousness of God in Christ.

That means that we can stand in the Father's presence with the same liberty and freedom that Jesus had.

Before that time, we had a sin-consciousness developed in us by spiritual death. Now we have Eternal Life-consciousness.

We are the Sons and Daughters of God. We have been growing in righteousness-consciousness and we are beginning to take our place and act the part of Sons and Daughters.

As we act on the Word, we have experience in Righteousness.

How vitally necessary it is that we become experienced in the Word which has taught us about Righteousness and taking our place in Righteousness.

I wonder if you understand what I mean?

You see, when Jesus began His public ministry, He was really the Righteousness of God unveiled.

Jesus had no sense of sin, no sense of inferiority.

He was a super-man. He was a Master of demons.

He was a Master of disease and sickness.

He was a Master of want and of hunger.

Well, when you and I came into Christ, He became our Righteousness, and then by the New Creation we became the Righteousness of God in Him.

We were not taught about our Righteousness.

We were not taught about our freedom in Christ.

We didn't know we were the masters of demons in the Name of Jesus.

We didn't know we had authority over all the authority of the enemy.

We didn't know that we could stand in the Father's presence just as freely as Jesus did, with no sense of inferiority, no sense of unworthiness, that we were the very Sons and Daughters of God.

Jesus wasn't afraid of the adversary.

That is one of the things that startled me in those early days of my study.

Jesus could walk into the presence of the devil without any fear.

He wasn't afraid when He stood beside the tomb of dead Lazarus, but you know, I was frightened for Him.

In my imagination I stood there. It was such a vivid scene, and I watched the Master as the crowd gathered, and I heard Him say with a loud voice, "Roll the stone away!"

Then my heart whispered softly, "Master, you had better go slow now; he has been in the tomb four days; he has been dead nearly a week. Martha has told you that his body decayeth," – but He interrupted my thinking and cried again, "Lazarus! Come forth."

Martha tried to intercept but it was too late. Jesus said, "Loose him and let him go," and out of the sepulchre came the man whose body was decaying.

Why was Jesus so fearless? Because He was the Righteousness of God. That is all.

He had no sense of sin. He had no sense of condemnation.

If the believer knew that he was the Righteousness of God as Jesus knew He was, he would use the Name of Jesus with a fearlessness that would startle hell and bless humanity.

Jesus said after He arose from the dead, "All authority has been given unto me in heaven and in earth; I am the head of the Church.

"Now I give you the legal right to use my Name, and all this authority is in that Name. In my name ye shall cast out demons.

"You see, I have given you authority over Satan.

"I have given you dominion over all the work that he has done.

"I came," said the Master, "to destroy the works of the devil.

"I am leaving it in your hands now."

If a believer becomes Righteousness-conscious, Son-conscious, Satan will be afraid of him.

Satan knows that as soon as the Church becomes conscious of the Reality of Redemption, that moment his reign over the earth is interrupted.

Jesus would never have given us the invitation in Heb. 4:16, to come boldly to the throne of grace, unless He had expected us to take our place and to act the part that belonged to us.

You see, we are what He says we are.

We should learn to use that Name as we use our own. To use prayer as we use an automobile.

As soon as we think through on these great problems they will become ours.

The trouble is, they have been taught us as doctrines.

They have been a part of a creed that we have believed, and most of us have joined a creedal church.

That creed has locked Jesus up so that He is helpless, and has locked us into a world conformity that makes us useless.

The thing He is trying to do these days is to make us free, to loose us from the bondage that has held us these years.

The Pauline Revelation is not a set of doctrines. It is just the Father speaking to us through Paul, unveiling what belongs to us in Christ.

Chapter XXII
THE REST OF REDEMPTION

EW of us know the reality of the Rest mentioned in Heb. 4:1: "Let us fear therefore, lest haply, a promise being left of entering into his rest, any one of you should seem to have come short of it."

When Jesus had finished His work, He sat down at the right hand of the Majesty on High. (Heb. 1:3).

Also Heb. 8:1: "Now in the things which we are saying, the chief point is this: We have such a high priest, who sat down on the right hand of the throne of the Majesty in the heavens."

Also Heb. 10:12, "But he, when he had offered one sacrifice for sins for ever, sat down on the right hand of God."

He had finished His work.

His work was wrought for us, not for Himself.

He entered into His rest.

And in Heb. 4:3 "For we who have believed do enter into that rest."

And in Heb. 4:11 "Let us therefore give diligence to enter into that rest, that no man fall after the same example of disobedience (or unpersuadableness)."

That is the rest of Faith. It is the end of worry and struggle.

You no longer seek for faith or power.

You have become one with Him.

You have come to appreciate the work that He did for you, and the work that the Holy Spirit, through the Word, has done in you.

You have come to know that you are what He says you are in Him.

You know that you are a New Creation.

You know that you have passed from death unto life.

You know that you have the very Life and Nature of the Father in you.

You know that, as He is now at the right hand of the Father, you are down here on earth.

You know that you are a part of the Body, a member of it.

You know that you were raised together with Him.

You know that no matter what may come to your life, you are more than a conqueror.

These are facts that you know.

You now enter into His Rest, the Rest that He purchased for you. You have reached the end of the worry route.

You are now so completely Identified with Him, so utterly one with Him, that the Father looks upon you as He looks upon His First Begotten, and because of that, peace that passeth all understanding fills your very being.

You remember Phil. 4:6,7. We ought to become thorough masters of that Scripture, and that Scripture should become our master. Notice what it says: "In nothing be anxious."

You see, you are in a place of rest.

"But in everything by prayer and supplication with thanksgiving, let your requests be made known unto God."

Why are you full of thanksgiving? Why is your heart filled with peace and rest? Why are you so joyful?

Because you know that whatsoever you ask the Father in Jesus' Name He will give it you.

Even to Israel He said, "Call unto me and I will answer you and show you great and mighty things which thou knowest not."

You are not under the Law; you are a Son.

You are an heir; you are a member of the Body, and He has invited you to come boldly to the Throne of Grace, and you have accustomed yourself to standing in His presence.

So now you are not anxious; you have believed.

I know the child is sick. The doctors have given him up to die, but you prayed for him.

Your heart is filled with thanksgiving and you are praising the Father.

Your relatives and loved ones can't understand you.

They whisper that Mother is beside herself.

You are not; you are beside the Master. The "Lo, I am with you always" is a reality to you.

You have entered into your Rest.

You know that no word from God is void of fulfillment, and that in every word there is Ability to make good.

You have prayed and you thank Him for the answer. "The answer is just as sure as the sun is to shine in the morning.

You have made your requests known unto the Father and now the miracle happens.

The peace of God which passeth all understanding has taken possession of your heart and your thoughts in Christ Jesus.

You haven't a thought of worry or care.

You haven't a burden.

I Pet. 5:7 illustrates this perfectly: "Casting all your anxiety upon him, because he careth for you."

You are not interested in the roaring of the adversary, nor the questioning of your friends, or the doubts of other people.

You know that your expectation is from Him.

You rest on His Word.

You have entered into His Rest.

When Jesus prayed, that settled it. There was no more talk about it. The answer had to come.

"Whatsoever ye ask the Father in my name, he will give it you."

That settles it.

You asked, didn't you? Well, the answer is on the way.

You are careful for nothing now.

You know that you and the Father are working together.

They can't fence you in with circumstances.

Phil. 4:11-13, "No, I have learned in whatever condition I am, to be independent of circumstances.

"I am schooled to bear the depths of poverty, I am schooled to bear abundance.

"In life as a whole, and in all its circumstances, I have mastered the secret of living – how to be the same amidst repletion and starvation, amidst abundance and privation.

"I am equal to every lot, through the help of Him who gives me strength." (Way Trans.)

You see, you have come into the place where circumstances no longer terrify, where the word of man is but the word of man to you.

The word of a doctor is only the word based on sense evidence.

The Word of God liveth and abideth. "No word from God is void of fulfillment."

The Word of God is speaking to you.

To you, the Word and God are one.

You haven't learned to separate Jesus from His words.

"The words that I speak, they are Spirit and they are Life." That is, they deal with your spirit nature and they give life and victory and peace and rest to your soul.

You are resting in the word.

Once you rested in the word of man, but you found that there was no rest for you.

Now you are resting in His Rest.

You see, it is the end of the fear of Satan, for he has been defeated.

It is the end of the fear of sickness, for by His stripes you are healed.

It is the end of lack; you fear it no longer. "Your heavenly Father knoweth that ye have need of all these things."

Want and fear have stopped being as far as you are concerned.

You never think of your weakness, for Jesus has become your ability.

The Greater One is living in you.

It is the end of ignorance. You have studied the Pauline Revelation until it has become a part of your knowledge, of your very life.

Col. 1:9-12 in the translation I am giving you now, should be a part of your life. It says, "I do not cease to pray and make request for you that ye may be filled with the exact knowledge of his will in all spiritual wisdom and understanding."

Can you see the breadth of that?

You know His will. You are filled with "exact knowledge" of the Father's will in all your life.

You are filled with Wisdom to use the Knowledge that you have gained in your study of the Word.

That Wisdom has enabled you to walk worthy unto the Lord in all pleasing.

You have reached the place where you are bearing fruit in every good work.

It is the fruit of Righteousness. You have become skilled in the Word of Righteousness.

You know your rights and privileges before the Throne, and you have Faith's fearlessness to enter the Father's presence any time, anywhere, and make your requests known.

You lounge around in the Throne Room visiting with the Father and Jesus.

You are more familiar with your Father and Jesus than you are with those with whom you have associated for years.

I hear your heart whisper, "I know Him in whom I have believed."

Now you walk worthy of the Lord and you are pleasing Him.

You have become a Father pleaser as Jesus was. (John 8:29).

"I please the Father in all that I do," saith the Master.

You are increasing, as you study the Word, in that Exact Knowledge of the Father.

It is a wonderful life you are living because the Wonder One is in you.

The Wonder One is your Teacher.

But hear the 11th verse: "Made strong with His ability according to the might of his glory."

This has given you steadfastness.

Where other people are breaking down and going to pieces, you are steadfast; you are immovable. You are always abounding in the work of the Lord.

You are strengthened for long-suffering.

People can't understand how you put up with things.

You whisper to them, "All things work together for good to me because I am in His will, and the very circumstances that rob you of your rest, increase my rest.

"The very opposition that destroyed your faith, builds mine; and you can't understand why I am filled with joy unspeakable and full of glory.

"He and I are laboring together.

"I am a partaker of His Faith. I breath in His very Life."

There was a steadfastness and a quietness about Jesus that has stopped being a wonder to me.

It has become my very joy for I have entered into it, and I am increasing continually in this exact Knowledge of my rights and privileges in Christ.

This is the reason that "I am giving thanks unto the Father who has given me the Ability to enjoy my share of the inheritance of the saints in light."

You see, I not only enjoy it but I am able to tell others and give them a hunger after it, and then I am able to show them the secret of entering into it.

You remember Col. 2:2-3, don't you? "That their hearts may be comforted, they being knit together in love, and unto all riches of the full assurance of understanding."

The fulness of assurance. That is wonderful, isn't it?

That makes you think of Col. 2:9, "For in him dwelleth all the fulness of the Godhead bodily, and in him ye are made full" or complete.

He made me that way. I couldn't do it.

He took me over and He built His fulness, His completeness into me.

Now I am rejoicing in the "full assurance of understanding, that they may know the mystery of God, even Christ."

Now hear this third verse: "In whom are all the treasures of wisdom and knowledge hidden."

Now I am going to take you back to Prov. 20:27: "The spirit of man is the lamp of Jehovah, searching all his innermost parts."

All the treasures of Wisdom and Knowledge and Love and Grace are hidden treasure chambers of Christ. He lighted up my spirit as a lamp and I went down into the hidden treasure chambers of Christ, and I found the riches of His Grace.

I became an explorer of the hidden things in Christ, and His Light lighted the way into them.

Now I become a possessor of these riches. They are mine and I live in the fulness of my riches in Christ.

See, they belong to us. There is no place for poverty in Him.

The Father never made a weak Christian. He has no pleasure in our weakness.

Some of us have thought that all the trials that come to us are God-sent. They are not.

The Father doesn't need the devil to purify and beautify His own.

No, these trials and difficulties are all Satan-inspired, and God has given us Ability to know this now, and so we are taking our place and rebuking the author of our troubles and commanding him to leave us alone.

We have found a strange, sweet quietness in the heart of Love.

You see, we have entered into our Rest.

There is no unpersuadableness in our hearts.

No matter how big the thing, how difficult to human reasoning, how many times sense knowledge rejects it, I am persuaded by the very Living Word that He is able to lead me into all the riches of the finished work of Christ, and because I know this, I have yielded my spirit to the Lordship of Love.

I have allowed the Word to dwell in me richly, and I have come to know the Reality of these mighty Truths of Redemption.

Chapter XXIII

"IT IS FINISHED"

ERHAPS no one sentence from the lips of the Master has been more misunderstood than the one that He uttered on the cross – "It is finished."

Most of us have believed that He meant He had finished His Redemptive work, but that is not true.

His work as a Substitute was just beginning and it was not consummated until His blood was accepted in the Supreme Court of the Universe, and He had sat down at the right hand of the Majesty on High.

But you ask, What did He mean then by "It is finished"?

It meant that He had fulfilled the Abrahamic Covenant, of which He, you remember, was a part.

He was born of Abraham's stock.

He was circumcised as a child and came into the Abrahamic Covenant.

He had grown up under the laws that governed the Israelitish people, who were children of the Covenant.

There are only two real Covenants in the Word – the Old Covenant and the New – the Abrahamic Covenant and the New Covenant in Christ.

God cut that first Covenant with Abraham.

Why do we use the word "cut a covenant"? Because the Hebrew word means to "cut a covenant."

Nearly all covenants made between men as recorded in the Scripture and as observed among primitive peoples, were solemnized by blood-letting.

Stanley gives us graphic pictures of covenants that he cut with chieftains in the heart of Africa.

When preliminaries had been finished, Stanley's companion offered his wrist to the Priest, who made an incision.

The son of the Chief that was to be his representative, offered his wrist and blood was let.

Then the two wrists were rubbed together and each one tasted the blood of the other.

Now these two men became blood brothers. Stanley and that chieftain had become blood brothers by substitution.

In Africa, Stanley and Livingston both confessed that they had never known of a covenant solemnized like this to be broken.

For a man to break it, sealed his own death warrant, for the tribe would not permit him to live and curse them.

So the Abrahamic Covenant was the most sacred covenant known to primitive peoples.

Circumcision permitted them to come into the Covenant, for when a child was circumcised, the priest would touch that blood to his tongue and that child became a child of the Abrahamic Covenant.

When Israel had crossed the Red Sea and gone into the wilderness, God gave them a Law – the Ten Commandments.

It was the Law of the Covenant.

He gave them a priesthood because the Law was broken and it meant death to them.

So with the priesthood came Atonement – a covering for that broken law, for the Hebrew word translated Atonement means "to cover."

Really, it has no other significance.

Theologians have read all kinds of things into it, but it stands simply as a covering for Israel because they were spiritually dead.

They have broken the Law and it meant death to them if it were not covered.

So when Jesus came, His first work was to fulfill that Abrahamic Covenant and set it aside.

Next, the Priesthood and the sacrifice and the Law were fulfilled and set aside.

The Book of Hebrews covers this ground very clearly.

Romans and Galatians also prove beyond the shadow of a doubt that Jesus fulfilled that First Covenant, the Law, the Priesthood and the Sacrifices, so that when He hung on the cross He could say, "It is finished."

The work that was not finished until He sat down at the right hand of the Father, was His work as a Substitute.

He had to die for the sins under the First Covenant, and He had to die for our sins, so His Substitution points both ways – back to the inception of the Abrahamic Covenant, on to the Great White Throne judgment.

In other chapters in this book, we have shown you how we were Identified with Christ in His Substitution because He died as our Substitute.

He suffered as our Substitute.

Our iniquities and our diseases were laid upon Him.

He was made sin with our sin.

Theologians tell us that they were "reckoned to Him."

If they were only reckoned to Him, then Redemption is only reckoned to us and we are not Redeemed.

If Righteousness is only reckoned to us, then Eternal Life and the New Creation are only reckoned to us.

In 1 Cor. 15:3 it says He died for our sins: "For I delivered unto you first of all that which also I received: that Christ died for our sins according to the scriptures."

"Him who knew no sin He made to be sin on our behalf: that we might become the righteousness of God in Him." (2 Cor. 5:21.)

"But now apart from the law a righteousness of God hath been manifested, being witnessed by the law and the prophets; even the righteousness of God through faith in Jesus Christ unto all them that believe; for there is no distinction; for all have sinned, and fall short of the glory of God; being justified freely by His grace through the redemption that is in Christ Jesus: whom God sent forth to be a propitiation, through faith, in His blood, to show His righteousness because of the passing over of the sins done aforetime, in the forbearance of God; for the showing, I say, of His righteousness at this present season: that he might himself be just, and the justifier of him that hath faith in Jesus." (Rom. 3:21-26.)

This shows beyond the shadow of a doubt that Christ was actually our Substitute, took our place, paid the penalty of the sins under the First Covenant and met the demands of Justice for us so that the New Birth could become a legal fact.

(I wish you would read my book, "The Father and His Family," for there we clear up the problem of the legal side of the plan of Redemption as we cannot in this volume.)

He not only had made our Redemption and our Righteousness a legal fact, but He made it possible for God to Recreate us, take us into His Family, honor us as Sons and Daughters on legal grounds.

When Jesus said, "It is finished" on the cross, we can now understand very clearly that He had no reference whatever of dealing with the sin problem, the Redemption problem, and the putting to naught of Satan, as Paul tells us in Heb. 2:14.

I want you to understand clearly that there are three phases of Christ's work connected with our Redemption.

First, was His work that He wrought in His earth walk, dealing with the First Covenant and everything that pertained to it.

Second, His Substitutionary work that began when He was made sin on the cross and was consummated when He carried His blood into the Heavenly Holy of Holies and it was accepted there for us.

And third, His ministry today at the right hand of the Majesty on High.

That ministry has to deal with the preservation and care of the Church.

He is there as our great High Priest, as the Surety of the Covenant, as our Savior, as our Mediator, our Advocate, and our Lord.

Chapter XXIV

JESUS AT THE RIGHT HAND
OF THE FATHER

EVERAL times the Word tells us that Jesus sat down at the right hand of the Majesty on High.

Heb. 1:3 is a good illustration. "Who being the effulgence of his glory, and the very image of his substance, and upholding all things by the word of his power, when he had made substitution for sins, sat down on the right hand of the Majesty on high."

Again, in Heb. 8:1-2: "Now in the things which we are saying, the chief point is this: We have such a high priest, who sat down on the right hand of the throne of the Majesty in the heavens, a minister of the sanctuary, and of the true tabernacle, which the Lord pitched, not man."

There is another expression connected with His heavenly ministry that we ought to notice.

Heb. 9:12, this clause: "He entered in once for all into the holy place, having obtained eternal redemption."

It was a "once for all" ministry.

Heb. 7:27 gives us the same thought: "For this he did once for all, when he offered up himself."

These two expressions are connected with His heavenly ministry.

You remember there are two phases of Christ's ministry.

One is His Substitutionary work from the cross until He arose from the dead.

In those three days and three nights He settled the sin problem, conquered the adversary, made the New Birth a possibility, and made Righteousness available to every person who receives Eternal Life.

His work at the right hand of the Father is what we might call a manifold work.

We must learn to appreciate the value of His ministry now at the right hand of the Father on our behalf.

He unveiled it to me very clearly, that had Jesus stopped His work after He had done this great Substitutionary Ministry from the cross to His Resurrection, had it ended there, no one could ever have been saved.

The next step in the drama had to be the carrying of His blood into the Heavenly Holy of Holies and making the Eternal Redemption for us.

You remember in John 20, when Mary saw Him, she fell down at His feet and tried to grasp them.

Jesus said to her tenderly, "Touch me not for I am not yet ascended unto my Father."

What did He mean? He arose as the Lord High Priest.

You remember in Matt. 28:6, the angels said to the women who came to the sepulchre, "You seek Jesus who was crucified: he is not here for he is risen. Come, see the place where the Lord lay."

He died a Lamb, but He arose as the Lord.

Lordship means absolute mastery and dominion.

Jesus died in weakness; He arose with all the authority and power and majesty of Deity.

He had conquered the dark forces of Satan.

He had dealt with the sin problem and redeemed humanity.

He made Eternal Life a possibility and Sonship a glory.

Now He says to Mary, "Touch me not."

Why? He had not carried His blood into Heaven yet and sealed the document of our Redemption.

The claims of Justice had not been met.

Jesus Our High Priest

Heb. 2:17, "Wherefore it behooved him in all things to be made like unto his brethren, that he might become a merciful and faithful high priest in things pertaining to God, to make propitiation for the sins of the people."

The claims of Justice had to be met first.

God had to be vindicated before the Supreme Court of the Universe.

He had given His Son to Redeem the human race.

That Son had died as a Substitute.

He had risen as the Lord High Priest of a New Covenant.

You understand, He had fulfilled the Old Covenant and there had been the annulling of the Priesthood and the Law of the Sacrifices with the Old Covenant.

Now a New Covenant has come into being and there must be a new Priesthood.

There must be a New Law.

The old Priesthood was to deal with servants.

The new Priesthood is to deal with Sons.

The old Priesthood had the Ten Commandments called "The Law of Death."

The New Covenant has but one commandment, "The Law of Life."

John 13:34-35, "A new commandment give I unto you that ye love one another even as I have loved you."

Jesus As Mediator

The first ministry that Jesus took after He had carried His blood into the Heavenly Holy of Holies, was that of a Mediator.

Heb. 9:12 (I am giving you another translation of this wonderful Scripture): "Nor yet with the blood of goats and calves, but with his own blood, entered in once for all into the holy place, having obtained Eternal redemption."

He went in with His own blood and that blood is the seal upon the document of our Redemption."

Heb. 9:24 says, "He entered heaven itself now to appear before the face of God for us."

His High Priestly ministry is over, as far as our Redemption is concerned.

His work is finished.

He said "it is finished" on the cross, but that didn't have reference to His Substitutionary work.

That had reference to His finishing His work of fulfilling the First Covenant and everything that pertained to it.

The Priesthood, the Sacrifice, the Atonement and the Law – all that was finished.

They no longer were operative.

Now the temple can be destroyed: the Priesthood can cease to function, because their Covenant on which everything was founded has been fulfilled and set aside.

Jesus the Savior

The next office that Jesus fills is that of a Savior.

Titus 2:10-11, "Not purloining, but showing all good fidelity; that they may adorn the doctrine of God our Savior in all things. For the grace of God hath appeared, bringing salvation to all men."

Jesus is God's Savior.

Acts 4:12, "For there is no other name under heaven, that is given among men, whereby we must be saved."

No man can save himself.

No man can make himself Righteous or give to himself Eternal Life.

There is but one Savior – the man Christ Jesus, who gave Himself a ransom for us all.

He might be a Savior; He might be God's own Savior, but His work of salvation would be limited and of no real value unless there was a Mediator between God and man.

How often we hear in evangelistic meetings, an invitation to come to Jesus and get sins pardoned.

If the one who invites the unsaved understood the Glad Tidings, he would never speak like that.

It is not coming to Jesus but it is going to God through Jesus.

I Tim. 2:5, "For there is one God, one mediator also between God and men, himself man, Christ Jesus, who gave himself a ransom for all."

Until we recognize the Mediatorial ministry of Jesus, our ministry will be cramped.

No man can reach the Father but through Him.

John 14:6. "I am the way, the truth, and the Life. No one can reach the Father but through me."

Jesus there is magnifying His position as a Mediator.

What the sinner needs is Eternal Life and remission of his trespasses.

He must be made a New Creation, but he cannot approach God.

He has no standing with God.

When Adam sinned in the Garden, he forfeited his legal right of approach to God.

Jesus, by His great Substitutionary work, purchased the right to be the Mediator between the unapproachable God and the sin-ruled sinner.

When the unsaved man makes his approach today, he wants to reach God.

He wants Eternal Life.

He wants the wiping out of all his old sins.

Jesus sits there as the Mediator between God and man.

He can be touched with the feeling of the infirmities of that lost world for which He died.

The Intercessor

He is not only the Mediator between God and man, but the moment that the unsaved man accepts Him as his Savior, then He becomes his Intercessor.

151

How happy my heart was when I first knew this.

I had someone to pray for me that I knew the Father would hear.

I remember what Jesus said as He stood before the tomb of Lazarus (John 11:41): "And Jesus lifted up his eyes, and said, Father, I thank thee that thou heardest me. And I know that thou hearest me always."

I have someone now to vouch for me, someone who never forgets me.

Heb. 7:25, "Wherefore also he is able to save to the uttermost them that come unto God by him, seeing he ever liveth to make intercession for them."

Here is a precious fact. The Greek word that is used, "saved" here, is "Sozo," which can be translated "heal," and it is rightly used because sin is sickness.

Disease is sickness, and Jesus came to "Sozo" us out of the hand of the enemy.

Isn't it wonderful that He ever lives to make intercession for us; to heal us of physical and spiritual diseases; to restore our broken spirits and to hold us in the hour of temptation and trial?

Not only is Jesus our great Intercessor. I love to think of Him as a High Priestly Intercessor, but He is more than that.

Our Advocate

I John 2:1-2 says, "My little children, these things write I unto you that ye may not sin. And if any man sin, we have an Advocate with the Father, Jesus Christ the righteous."

That is a remarkable expression and it is a wonderful ministry.

There He sits at the right hand of the Father, as the sinner's Savior, as the believer's Mediator, but now the believer is out of fellowship.

The adversary has gained dominion over him. He is under condemnation.

It seems as though his heart would break, and then he remembers in the midst of his sorrow and grief that Jesus is his Advocate, his lawyer, who ever lives, not only to make intercession for him, but He is there to appear before the Father on his behalf.

So the believer lifts up his voice and cries, "Father, in Jesus' Name, forgive me," and his great Advocate whispers, "Father, lay that to my charge."

So everything is wiped out and once more he can stand before the Father without condemnation.

You see, He is called the Righteous Advocate, because the believer that has sinned has lost the sense of Righteousness and his Righteousness is of no avail to him as long as his heart is under condemnation.

Then he needs his Righteous Advocate, who can go into the Father's presence and make an appeal for him and restore that lost joy and the sense of Righteousness again.

You see, the present ministry of Jesus is of infinite value to the believer.

Jesus Our Lord

Not only is He Savior, Intercessor and Advocate, but He is our Lord and Head.

Col. 2:6-7, notice this translation: "As therefore ye received Christ Jesus the Lord, so walk in him, rooted and builded up in him, and established in your faith, even as ye were taught, abounding in thanksgiving."

I read that over and over many times.

That scripture was like a storehouse filled with priceless treasure, but I couldn't seem to get a key to it.

Then this translation came. Then I saw what it meant.

He wanted me to be rooted and established in the reality of the Lordship of Jesus over me.

When I first began to study about His Lordship, I was afraid of Him.

I had a feeling that it meant slavery to me, but it didn't.

It meant just what the 23rd Psalm says, "The Lord is my shepherd. I shall not want."

I like the other rendering better: "Jehovah is my Shepherd, I do not want."

Why? He maketh me to lie down in green pastures where food is abundant, where water is near me, where I am fully protected from the elements and from my enemies.

He is my present Shepherd Lord.

The word Lord means Bread-provider, Shield and Protector.

He is all that a husband can mean to his wife.

He is all that a lover can mean to his beloved.

The Father wants me to be rooted and grounded and built up in this blessed Truth.

He wants my faith to rest upon absolute certainty of the Lordship of Jesus over me.

Then my heart will be full of abounding joy and thanksgiving.

You see, until we know about the Lordship of Jesus at the right hand of the Father, there will never be that quiet restfulness in our spirit.

You can find that practically all the believers that are living beneath their privileges, are having a hard time in their spiritual life.

They have never been instructed in the ministry of Jesus at the right hand of the Father.

Years ago I held a blessed campaign in Moncton, N. B., Canada.

Months afterwards I returned for another campaign, and I asked the congregation, "What truth helped you the most?"

Many voices answered back, "Your teaching about Jesus' ministry at the right hand of the Father."

Jesus, the Surety of the New Covenant

He is not only our High Priest, Savior, Intercessor, Advocate and Lord, but there is another priceless ministry of my seated Lord.

He is the "Surety of the New Covenant."

Heb. 7:18, "For there is a disannulling of a foregoing commandment because of its weakness and unprofitableness (for the law made nothing perfect), and a bringing in thereupon of a better hope, through which we draw nigh unto God."

By a single stroke He has cleared up the issue of that First Covenant and the Law.

Because of their weakness they could not make men Righteous; they could not make men holy; they could not give Eternal Life.

Heb. 10:1-3 will throw much light on this. "For the law having a shadow of the good things to come, not the very image of the things, can never with the same sacrifices year by year, which they offer continually, make perfect them that draw nigh.

"Else would they not have ceased to be offered? because the worshippers, having been once cleansed, would have had no more consciousness of sins.

"But in those sacrifices there is a remembrance made of sin year by year.

"For it is impossible that the blood of bulls and goats should take away sins."

But there has come a New Covenant, and on the basis of that New Covenant we may be Born Again, born of Heaven, born of God, receive the Nature and Life of the Father God.

We may become the very Righteousness of God in Him.

Can anyone overestimate the value of such a Covenant?

This is a Covenant of Love, a Covenant of Life, a Covenant of the New Creation.

Heb. 7:20-24, "And inasmuch as it is not without the taking of an oath (for they indeed have been made priests without an oath; but he with an oath by him that saith of him, The Lord sware and will not repent himself, Thou art a priest forever)."

You see, Jesus was outside of the priestly family.

They became priests by being born into the priesthood naturally. The oldest son was always the High Priest.

But Jesus was a Priest by an oath of Jehovah.

"The Lord sware and will not repent himself, Thou art a priest forever."

Now notice this great sentence: "By so much also hath Jesus become the surety of a better covenant. And they indeed have been made priests many in number, because that by death they are hindered from continuing; but he, because he abideth forever, hath his priesthood unchangeable."

There is a priest who abideth forever as the surety of this New Covenant.

Back of this New Covenant then, what we call the New Testament, we have Jesus as its Surety.

From Matt. 1 to Rev. 22, Jesus and His throne are back of every word.

"No word from God can be void of fulfillment."

Now you can quote Jer. 1:12: "I watch over my word to fulfill it."

Jesus can say, "Heaven and earth can pass away, but my word can never pass away."

That is the Word of the New Covenant.

His blood is the red seal upon the document of this Covenant.

On the ground of the integrity of that indissoluble covenant, you and I can build a Faith that cannot be shaken.

"He Sat Down"

Now you can understand what this beautiful expression means that is used so many times in Hebrews – "He sat down."

We go back to Heb. 1:3 and feast our spirits upon it.

"Who, being the effulgence of his glory (or the very outshining of his glory), and the very image of his substance, and upholding all things by the word of his ability."

The word translated power means "ability.'"

All the ability of Deity is back of that Covenant.

Now notice carefully: "When he had made purification (or substitution) for sins, sat down on the right hand of the Majesty on high."

He is in the highest seat in the universe and holds the highest office in the universe, and He is my Lord.

He is the head of the Body, and "of His fulness have we all received, and grace upon grace."

How rich we are. We can never again talk of our lack of our weakness, of our unworthiness, because that great Substitutionary sacrifice that He wrought for us has guaranteed to us Eternal Life, and a standing with the Father, victory over our enemies, peace that passeth all understanding, joy beyond words.

All are ours because of what He is for us now at the right hand of the Majesty on High.

Chapter XXV

WHY NATURAL MAN CANNOT KNOW HIMSELF

MAN in the Garden lived in the realm of the spirit. He had perfect fellowship with God. His spirit dominated him.

Then sin came and he was driven from the presence of God. From that moment he lived under the domination of his senses.

These five senses became his master.

His spirit lost dominion the moment that he became spiritually dead, a partaker of Satan's nature.

This, you understand, happened when he sinned.

The real man is a spirit being, but the moment that spiritual death took possession of his spirit, his senses dominated.

He lost his approach to God the moment that he sinned.

The nature that he received made him antagonistic to God.

Rom. 8:7, "Because the mind of the senses is enmity against God; for it is not subject to the law of God, neither indeed can it be: so they that are governed by the senses cannot please God."

This translation of the Greek word Sarx to "senses'" instead of "flesh," gives us the true intent of the word.

You remember 1 Cor. 2:14 declares, "Now the natural man (the man of the senses) receiveth not the things of the Spirit of God: for they are foolishness unto him; and he cannot know them, because they are spiritually understood."

So when man fell and his spirit received the nature of the adversary, he really became a stranger to himself.

He is a spirit being and is no longer dominated by himself but by his body in which he lives.

It made him a slave to his body instead of a master over it.

You understand that when this thing happened in the Garden, he lost contact with God, lost his ability to approach Him, and he went out into the world to live by his senses.

We have a modern saying, that "man lives by his wits."

That is another way of expressing the same fact.

We know that man cannot contact God through his reasoning faculties; that his only contact with Him is with his spirit.

Having died spiritually, he is unable to make this contact.

It is very difficult for man's language to convey God's thought.

The Hebrew language is a dead language and it is a limited language.

We have many words for which the Hebrew language has no equivalent

For instance, the word "Ruach," translated spirit, can mean air, anger, blast, breath, cool, courage, mind, quarters, side, spirit, tempest, wind, vain, windy; and in one place it has been translated whirlwind.

By this you can see how limited the Hebrew language was to convey God's thoughts.

That is the reason why the word "Ruach," translated spirit, is often misunderstood by the sense knowledge of translators.

You remember that man's thoughts are not always God's thoughts.

Man was Love's product created to be His child and companion.

He was created in God's class of being, in His image and in His likeness.

God is Eternal. Man is Eternal.

God is a spirit. Man is a spirit.

Man was so Created that he could partake of God's Nature and become God's child.

Now mark this fact: Man cannot be spiritual unless he is a spirit.

He cannot know spiritual things unless he is a spirit.

He cannot partake of God's Nature unless he is in God's class of being.

You can understand now the calamity that befell man when his spirit lost control over his senses.

In that moment his senses governed his spirit.

All the knowledge that natural man has, has come through these five avenues of the body – seeing, hearing, tasting, smelling, feeling.

The brain has no capacity to think independent of sense evidences.

A child that is born without sight, or hearing, or feeling, would be called an imbecile, though its brain was as perfect as the brain of any child.

That brain had no contact with the world because the senses failed to function.

Now we can understand that man's physical contact is with the physical.

His mental contact is with the mental.

His spirit then can contact only the spiritual.

158

If man's reasoning faculties cannot contact God, then it is up to his spirit to make that contact.

Man's reasoning faculties are utterly dependent upon the senses.

Sense knowledge is unable to contact his spirit in any intelligent way until after that spirit has been Recreated, received the Nature of God, and his reasoning faculties have been renewed and brought into harmony with the Recreated spirit.

Now we can understand the difficulties of psychologists.

You understand this is a study of the mind of man, and if the psychologist doesn't know about the spirit of man, about what happened to the spirit of man in the Garden, he will be unable to approach this subject with any clarity of thought.

Most of our psychologists deny that man is a spirit. He is simply a psychical or soulical man.

He denies the existence of the spirit, and this denial makes it impossible for the spirit to function.

Now you can see why natural man cannot know himself, because he is a spirit.

The senses cannot register anything of the spirit or give him any spirit knowledge.

One who knows anatomy and physiology may not know much about the mind and he may not know man himself. All he knows is connected with the physical.

Natural man is in the same condition.

He cannot know spirit or spiritual things, so he cannot know himself, for he is spirit.

This is the reason that modern psychology is ofttimes misleading.

Modern psychologists are majoring functional psychology or psychology based on the study of the five senses and their reaction upon the mind.

The New Creation man finds a new self in Christ, and that new self becomes almost independent of the senses when he comes into closest fellowship with the Father.

"Wherefore, if any man is in Christ, he is a New Creation," a new self.

The real self has been made anew, Recreated.

That means his spirit has been Recreated.

It is imperative now that the mind which derives all of its impulses, all of its knowledge from the five senses, should come under the dominion of this new Recreated spirit or self.

This can only come as man begins to study the Word and then begins to practice and live it.

It is a fact of great importance that every believer should know, that there is no such thing as understanding the Word until the mind is renewed.

The reason for that is, that the Word is the work of the Holy Spirit and it is a spiritual thing, and sense knowledge cannot understand spiritual things.

So it is necessary that his mind be renewed and come into fellowship with his spirit.

It is almost imperative that this Recreated spirit should gain the dominance over his reasoning faculties.

You know how we often fight our conscience, and how it is often in opposition to our reasoning faculties.

That conscience is the voice of our spirit.

If we should learn to obey our conscience we could walk continuously in fellowship with the Word and with the Father; but the reason is, we have not learned to give our spirit the place of authority and dominion that belongs to it.

Educating Our Spirits

This brings us to another phase of this study.

Your spirit can be educated just as really as the mind is educated.

It can be built up in strength just as the body can be built up.

That comes by meditation in the Word.

By practicing the Word.

By giving the Word the first place.

By instantly obeying the voice of our spirit.

After awhile you can know the will of the Father in all the details of life, because He communicates with your spirit, not with the reasoning faculties.

You know Paul speaks of the mind of the spirit.

Rom. 8:6, "For the mind of the senses leads us into the realm of spiritual death, but the mind of the spirit (that is our Recreated spirit) leads us into the realm of life and peace."

The Life there is "Zoe"– Eternal Life – the Nature of God.

The spirit mentioned here is the Recreated spirit, not the Holy Spirit.

It is hard for us to accept the fact that the natural man is ruled by the five senses.

His body is the teacher of his mind and he cannot grow in knowledge beyond the reactions of his senses upon his brain.

The New Creation man has almost an unlimited opportunity of growth because his spirit has received the Nature of God.

He is in perfect fellowship with his Father.

He has an unlimited use of the name of Jesus that the natural man does not have.

He has the Wisdom of God, for Jesus is made unto him Wisdom. Natural man has nothing but the Wisdom that comes to him through his unrecreated spirit.

The New Creation man has the ability of God at his disposal.

You see, he is lifted out of the natural realm into the spiritual realm, and when he is Recreated, he has the privilege of having the Holy Spirit, who raised Jesus from the Dead, to come and make His home in his body.

Now you can understand Rom. 12:1-2, "I beseech you therefore, brethren, by the mercies of God, to present your bodies a living sacrifice, holy, acceptable to God, which is your spiritual worship.

"And be not fashioned according to this age: but be ye transfigured by the renewing of your mind, that ye may prove what is the good and well-pleasing and perfect will of God." (Free translation.)

This shows us why it is imperative to have the body, the university of the mind, under the control of the Recreated spirit.

This New Creation man does not walk under the dominion of the senses but is to be governed by the Word of God.

It is going to be hard for us to see that this physical body of ours is not only the home of the five senses, but that these five senses have been the instructors and teachers of the brain.

That makes the body the university of the brain.

The five senses are the instructors.

This body is the laboratory where the brain receives all of its instructions.

These senses are five avenues to the brain, for we know that the brain cannot function without the senses.

Here are some facts that may be hard to assimilate.

The brain has no creative ability.

It has nothing of itself by which it can create.

It is dependent upon these five instructors.

The brain, by much training, can advise what action is best after the senses have communicated, but if the senses never function, the brain will never develop.

As long as the natural human spirit is held in bondage by spiritual death it has no creative ability.

This can be seen in heathen countries where they have never received Eternal Life.

Spiritually dead men in those countries have no creative ability.

They may be able to follow blue prints; they can imitate; they can experiment as they do in chemistry, but it must end there.

Man's creative ability is not in the reasoning faculties.

Reader, can't you see the imperative need of giving to the youth of our nation Eternal Life?

I have proven to you in another chapter, that the children who have received Eternal Life in the teen age, seldom sow wild oats; seldom ever become criminals.

They are easier to rear and to control, and they are more responsive to the appeal of the Word of God.

Another fact: Inventors know this to be true, that after hours of experimenting, their minds are worn and tired.

They stop to rest, and suddenly, without any effort, the thing they have been searching for flashes into their mind.

They know not from whence it came, but it has arrived.

What did it? Their Spirit spoke as soon as the reasoning faculties were silent and it could be heard.

Sometimes it comes in a dream or in the early morning when first awaking.

Psychologists have been puzzled by this. They had no answer for what seemed to them a mystery, so they called that something a "sub-conscious mind."

But we of the New Creation know there is no such thing as a sub-conscious mind; it is the mind of the spirit.

It is the spirit struggling to express itself.

But you ask, can't the natural man cultivate his spirit?

Yes, but it will be the cultivation of a spirit dominated by spiritual death.

That has given to us spiritualism with all those dangerous cults from India; given to us the strange miracles of the occult that often imitate God.

Here are more facts of vital importance.

The Recreated spirit becomes the fountain of all the beautiful things that Christianity has given to us.

Gal. 5:22-25, "But the fruit of the spirit is love, joy, peace,

INSPIRING BOOKS BY E. W. KENYON

THE BIBLE IN THE LIGHT OF OUR REDEMPTION
A Basic Bible Course

ADVANCED BIBLE COURSE
Studies in the Deeper Life

THE HIDDEN MAN OF THE HEART

WHAT HAPPENED
From the Cross to the Throne

NEW CREATION REALITIES

IN HIS PRESENCE
The Secret of Prayer

THE TWO KINDS OF LIFE

THE FATHER AND HIS FAMILY
The Story of Man's Redemption

THE WONDERFUL NAME OF JESUS
Our Rights and Privileges in Prayer

JESUS THE HEALER
Has Brought Healing to Thousands

KENYON'S LIVING POEMS

THE NEW KIND OF LOVE

THE TWO KINDS OF FAITH

THE TWO KINDS OF RIGHTEOUSNESS

THE BLOOD COVENANT

THE TWO KINDS OF KNOWLEDGE

SIGN POSTS ON THE ROAD TO SUCCESS

IDENTIFICATION

Order From:
KENYON'S GOSPEL PUBLISHING SOCIETY
P.O. Box 973, Lynnwood, Washington 98046-0973
website: www.kenyons.org